BEGINNING
ETHICS

An Introduction to Moral Philosophy

BEGINNING ETHICS

An Introduction to Moral Philosophy

LEWIS VAUGHN

W. W. NORTON & COMPANY, INC.

NEW YORK · LONDON

W. W. NORTON & COMPANY has been independent since its founding in 1923, when Wiliam Warder Norton and Mary D. Herter Norton first published lectures delivered at the People's Institute, the adult education division of New York City's Cooper Union. The firm soon expanded its program beyond the Institute, publishing books by celebrated academics from America and abroad. By midcentury, the two major pillars of Norton's publishing program—trade books and college texts—were firmly established. In the 1950s, the Norton family transferred control of the company to its employees, and today—with a staff of four hundred and a comparable number of trade, college, and professional titles published each year—W. W. Norton & Company stands as the largest and oldest publishing house owned wholly by its employees.

Editor: Peter Simon

Associate Editor: Quynh Do

Manuscript Editor: JoAnn Simony

Project Editor: Sujin Hong

Production Manager: Ben Reynolds

Text Design: Rubina Yeh

Composition: Cathy Lombardi

Manufacturing: RR Donnelley-Harrisonburg, VA

The text of this book is composed in Stone Serif ITC Std Medium with the display set in Syndor ITC Std Book.

Library of Congress Cataloging-in-Publication Data

Vaughn, Lewis, author.
  Beginning ethics: an introduction to moral philosophy / Lewis Vaughn. -- First edition.
    pages cm
Includes bibliographical references and index.
  ISBN 978-0-393-93790-9 (pbk.)
1. Ethics--Textbooks. I. Title.
BJ1025.V38 2015
170--dc23
                          2014020838

W. W. Norton & Company, Inc., 500 Fifth Avenue, New York, N.Y. 10110

W. W. Norton & Company, Ltd., Castle House, 75/76 Wells Street, London W1T 3QT

wwnorton.com

1 2 3 4 5 6 7 8 9 0

CONTENTS

Preface   11

CHAPTER 1 Ethics and the Moral Life   13

The Ethical Landscape   16

The Elements of Ethics   18

    THE PREEMINENCE OF REASON   19

    THE UNIVERSAL PERSPECTIVE   19

    THE PRINCIPLE OF IMPARTIALITY   20

    THE DOMINANCE OF MORAL NORMS   21

Religion and Morality   21

    BELIEVERS NEED MORAL REASONING   22

    WHEN CONFLICTS ARISE, ETHICS STEPS IN   23

    MORAL PHILOSOPHY ENABLES PRODUCTIVE DISCOURSE   23

Keywords   26

Exercises   26

    REVIEW QUESTIONS   26

    ESSAY QUESTIONS   27

Ethical Dilemmas   27

CHAPTER 2 Relativism and Emotivism   29

Subjective Relativism   31

Cultural Relativism   32

Emotivism   40

Keywords   43

Exercises   44
    REVIEW QUESTIONS   44
    ESSAY QUESTIONS   44
Ethical Dilemmas   45

CHAPTER 3 Moral Arguments   46
Claims and Arguments   47
Arguments Good and Bad   51
Implied Premises   56
Moral Statements and Arguments   58
Testing Moral Premises   62
Assessing Nonmoral Premises   65
Avoiding Bad Arguments   66
    BEGGING THE QUESTION   67
    EQUIVOCATION   67
    APPEAL TO AUTHORITY   68
    SLIPPERY SLOPE   68
    APPEAL TO EMOTION   69
    FAULTY ANALOGY   69
    APPEAL TO IGNORANCE   70
    STRAW MAN   71
    APPEAL TO THE PERSON   71
    HASTY GENERALIZATION   72
Keywords   72
Exercises   74
    REVIEW QUESTIONS   74
    ESSAY QUESTIONS   75
    ARGUMENT EXERCISES   75
Ethical Dilemmas   76

CHAPTER 4 Moral Theories   78
Theories of Right and Wrong   78
Major Theories   81
    CONSEQUENTIALIST THEORIES   81
    NONCONSEQUENTIALIST THEORIES   82

Evaluating Theories 84
    CRITERION 1: CONSISTENCY WITH
    CONSIDERED JUDGMENTS 86
    CRITERION 2: CONSISTENCY WITH OUR
    MORAL EXPERIENCE 87
    CRITERION 3: USEFULNESS IN MORAL
    PROBLEM SOLVING 88
Keywords 89
Exercises 90
    REVIEW QUESTIONS 90
    ESSAY QUESTIONS 90
Ethical Dilemmas 91

CHAPTER 5 Ethical Egoism 92
Applying the Theory 94
Evaluating the Theory 96
Keywords 101
Exercises 101
    REVIEW QUESTIONS 101
Ethical Dilemmas 101

CHAPTER 6 Utilitarianism 103
Applying the Theory 109
Evaluating the Theory 110
Learning from Utilitarianism 117
Keywords 117
Exercises 118
    REVIEW QUESTIONS 118
Ethical Dilemmas 118

CHAPTER 7 Kantian Ethics 120
Applying the Theory 125
Evaluating the theory 126
Learning from Kant's Theory 129

Keywords   129
Exercises   130
   REVIEW QUESTIONS   130
Ethical Dilemmas   130

CHAPTER 8 Natural Law Theory   132
Applying the Theory   135
Evaluating the Theory   137
Learning from Natural Law   138
Keyword   139
Exercises   139
   REVIEW QUESTIONS   139
Ethical Dilemmas   140

CHAPTER 9 Social Contract Theory   141
Hobbes's Theory   142
Pluses and Minuses   144
Keyword   146
Exercises   146
   REVIEW QUESTIONS   146
Ethical Dilemmas   147

CHAPTER 10 The Feminist Challenge   148
Feminist Ethics   149
The Ethics of Care   151
Keywords   152
Exercises   152
   REVIEW QUESTIONS   152
   ESSAY QUESTIONS   153
Ethical Dilemmas   153

CHAPTER 11 Virtue Ethics   155
Virtue in Action   157
Evaluating Virtue Ethics   158
Learning from Virtue Ethics   161

Keywords   162
Exercises   163
  REVIEW QUESTIONS   163
Ethical Dilemmas   163

CHAPTER 12 A Moral Theory   165
Moral Common Sense   165
Building a Moral Theory   166
Prima Facie Principles   167
Three Rules   169
Self-Evidence   174
Keywords   176
Exercises   176
  REVIEW QUESTIONS   176
  ESSAY QUESTIONS   177
Ethical Dilemmas   177

Further Reading   179
Glossary   185
Index   189

PREFACE

This book does what any good ethics text of this kind should do, and perhaps a little more. It introduces students to basic ethical concepts (principles, virtues, values, and the like), reviews the major moral theories and arguments, critiques relativism and moral skepticism, and explains why ethics matters to students and to the world. But it also tries to take into account two barriers to ethical understanding: (1) that students approaching ethics for the first time may find it disorienting, confusing, intimidating, perhaps even annoying (because the ideas discussed may conflict with their own); and (2) that students may have no inkling of how to apply what they learn about moral philosophy to their lives.

To address the first challenge, this text presents the material as clearly and as approachably as possible without dumbing down complex ideas and thorny problems. Moreover, students' preconceptions (many of them unsupportable)—preconceptions about the nature of ethics, morality and religion, moral and nonmoral claims, morality and feelings, morality and reason, moral relativism and emotivism, and moral deliberation—are addressed head on. After reading these direct challenges to their uninformed views, students may or may not change their minds about them. But they won't be able to say they don't understand why ethics is regarded as a subject worthy of serious study and discussion.

The second challenge is dealt with through a strong emphasis on critical reasoning in the moral life. A key underlying message is that students are already in the thick of ethical quandaries and decision-making in their daily lives. What this book offers students is a framework for navigating these waters more consciously and deliberately. A full chapter is devoted to critical thinking as applied to ethics—that is, to understanding and evaluating moral arguments, premises, judgments, cases, and principles. Another chapter explores the nature of moral theories and how they relate to other elements in moral deliberations. The aim of this chapter is to demonstrate how moral theories are applied in the real world and how they are critically examined using widely accepted criteria of adequacy.

In addition, each chapter contains exercises in several forms—a feature that sets this book apart from other texts of its kind. Every chapter provides review questions, and Chapters 1 through 4 and 10 and 12 also have essay questions. Chapter 3 (Moral Arguments) adds argument exercises to the mix. (The argument exercises help students hone their skills in evaluating and formulating moral arguments.) And all chapters end with a set of "ethical dilemmas"—scenarios that provide practice in applying moral concepts and theories to actual cases. The idea underlying the end-of-chapter scenarios is that one of the best ways to learn how to apply moral concepts and theories is through practice. And practice leads to a better appreciation of some of the complexities of the moral life and the potent utility of moral reasoning.

CHAPTER 1

Ethics and the Moral Life

Ethics, or **moral philosophy**, is the philosophical study of morality. **Morality** refers to beliefs concerning right and wrong, good and bad—beliefs that can include judgments, values, rules, principles, and theories. These beliefs help guide our actions, define our values, and give us reasons for being the persons we are. Ethics, then, addresses the powerful question that Socrates formulated twenty-four hundred years ago: How ought we to live?

The continued relevance of this query suggests something compelling about ethics: you cannot escape it. You cannot run away from all of the choices, feelings, and actions that accompany ideas about right and wrong, good and bad—ideas that persist in your culture and in your mind. After all, for much of your life, you have been assimilating, modifying, or rejecting the ethical norms you inherited from your family, community, and society. Unless you are very unusual, from time to time you deliberate about the rightness or wrongness of actions, embrace or reject particular moral principles or codes, judge the goodness of your character or intentions (or someone else's), perhaps even question (and agonize over) the soundness of your own moral outlook when it conflicts with that of others. In other words, you are involved in ethics—you *do* ethics—throughout your life. Even if you try to remove yourself from the ethical realm by insisting that all ethical concepts are irrelevant or empty, you will have assumed a particular view—a theory in the broadest sense—about morality and its place in your life. If at some point you are intellectually brave enough to wonder whether your moral beliefs rest on coherent supporting considerations, you will see that you cannot even begin to sort out such considerations without—again—doing ethics. In any case, in your life you must deal with the rest of the world, which turns on moral conflict and resolution, moral decision and debate.

What is at stake when we do ethics? In an important sense, the answer is *everything we hold dear*. Ethics is concerned with values—specifically, *moral values*. Through the sifting and weighing of moral values we determine what the most important things are in our lives, what is worth living for and what is worth dying for. We decide what is the greatest good, what goals we should pursue in life, what virtues we should cultivate, what duties we should fulfill, what value we should put on human life, and what pain and perils we should be willing to endure for notions such as the common good, justice, and rights.

Does it matter whether the state executes criminals who have the mental capacity of a ten-year-old? Does it matter whether we can easily save a starving child but casually decide not to? Does it matter who actually writes the term paper you turn in and represent as your own? Does it matter whether young girls in Africa have their genitals painfully mutilated for reasons of custom or religion? Do these actions and a million others just as controversial matter at all? Most of us—regardless of our opinion on these issues—would say that they matter a great deal. If they matter, then ethics matters, because these are ethical concerns requiring careful reflection using concepts and reasoning peculiar to ethics.

But even though ethics is inescapable and important in life, you are still free to take the easy way out, and many people do. You are free *not* to think too deeply or too systematically about ethical concerns. You can simply embrace the moral beliefs and norms given to you by your family and your society. You can just accept them without question or serious examination. In other words, you can try *not* to do ethics. This approach can be simple and painless—at least for a while—but it has some drawbacks.

First, it undermines your personal freedom. If you accept and never question the moral beliefs handed to you by your culture, then those beliefs are not really yours—and they, not you, control your path in life. Only if you critically examine these beliefs *yourself* and decide for *yourself* whether they have merit will they be truly yours. Only then will you be in charge of your own choices and actions. The philosopher John Stuart Mill summed up the ask-no-questions approach to life pretty well: "He who lets the world, or his own portion of it, choose his plan of life for him, has no need of any other faculty than the ape-like one of imitation."[1]

Second, the morally blind attitude increases the chance that your responses to moral dilemmas or contradictions will be incomplete, confused, or mistaken. Sometimes in real life, moral codes or rules do not fit the situations at hand, or moral principles conflict with one another, or entirely new circumstances are not covered by any moral policy at all. Solving these problems requires something that a hand-me-down morality does not include: the intellectual tools to critically evaluate (and reevaluate) existing moral beliefs.

Third, if there is such a thing as intellectual moral growth, you are unlikely to find it on the safe route. To not do ethics is to stay locked in a kind of intellectual limbo in which personal moral progress is barely possible.

The philosopher Paul Taylor suggests that there is yet another risk in taking the easy road. If someone blindly embraces the morality bequeathed to him by his society, he may very well be a fine embodiment of the rules of his culture and accept them with certainty. But he also will lack the ability to defend his beliefs by rational argument against criticism. What happens when he encounters others who also have very strong beliefs that contradict his? "He will feel lost and bewildered," Taylor says, and his confusion might leave him disillusioned about morality. "Unable to give an objective, reasoned justification for his own convictions, he may turn from dogmatic certainty to total skepticism. And from total skepticism it is but a short step to an 'amoral' life. . . . Thus the person who begins by accepting moral beliefs blindly can end up denying all morality."[2]

There are other easy roads—roads that also bypass critical and thoughtful scrutiny of morality. We can describe most of them as various forms of subjectivism, a topic that we closely examine later on. You may decide, for example, that you can establish all your moral beliefs by simply consulting your feelings. In situations calling for moral judgments, you let your emotions be your guide. If it feels right, it is right. Alternatively, you may come to believe that moral realities are relative to each person, a view known as *subjective relativism* (also covered in a later chapter). That is, you think that what a person believes or approves of determines the rightness or wrongness of actions. If you believe that abortion is wrong, then it *is* wrong. If you believe it is right, then it *is* right.

But these facile pathways through ethical terrain are no better than blindly accepting existing norms. Even if you want to take the subjectivist route, you still need to critically examine it to see if there are good reasons for choosing it—otherwise your choice is arbitrary and therefore not really yours. And unless you thoughtfully consider the merits of moral beliefs (including subjectivist beliefs), your chances of being wrong about them are substantial.

Ethics does not give us a royal road to moral truth. Instead, it shows us how to ask critical questions about morality and systematically seek answers supported by good reasons. This is a tall order because, as we have seen, many of the questions in ethics are among the toughest we can ever ask—and among the most important in life.

THE ETHICAL LANDSCAPE

The domain of ethics is large, divided into several areas of investigation, and cordoned off from related subjects. So let us map the territory carefully. As the term *moral philosophy* suggests, ethics is a branch of philosophy. A very rough characterization of philosophy is the systematic use of critical reasoning to answer the most fundamental questions in life. Moral philosophy, obviously, tries to answer the fundamental questions of morality. The other major philosophical divisions address other basic questions; these are *logic* (the study of correct reasoning), *metaphysics* (the study of the fundamental nature of reality), and *epistemology* (the study of knowledge). As a division of philosophy, ethics does its work primarily through critical reasoning. Critical reasoning is the careful, systematic evaluation of statements, or claims—a process used in all fields of study, not just in ethics. Mainly this process includes both the evaluation of logical arguments and the careful analysis of concepts.

Science also studies morality, but not in the way that moral philosophy does. Its approach is known as **descriptive ethics**—the *scientific* study of moral beliefs and practices. Its aim is to describe and explain how people actually behave and think when dealing with moral issues and concepts. This kind of empirical research is usually conducted by sociologists, anthropologists, and psychologists. In contrast, the focus of moral philosophy is not what people actually believe and do, but what they *should* believe and do. The point of moral philosophy is to determine what actions are right (or wrong) and what things are good (or bad).

Philosophers distinguish three major divisions in ethics, each one representing a different way to approach the subject. The first is **normative ethics**—the study of the principles, rules, or theories that guide our actions and judgments. (The word *normative* refers to norms, or standards, of judgment—in this case, norms for judging rightness and goodness.) The ultimate purpose of doing normative ethics is to try to establish the soundness of moral norms, especially the norms embodied in a comprehensive moral system, or theory. We do normative ethics when we use critical reasoning to demonstrate that a moral principle is justified, or that a professional code of conduct is contradictory, or that one proposed moral theory is better than another, or that a person's motive is good. Should the rightness of actions be judged by their consequences? Is happiness the greatest good in life? Is utilitarianism a good moral theory? Such questions are the preoccupation of normative ethics.

Another major division is **metaethics**—the study of the meaning and logical structure of moral beliefs. It asks not whether an action is right or whether a person's character is good. It takes a step back from these concerns and asks more fundamental questions about them: What does it mean for an action to be *right*? Is *good* the same thing as *desirable*? How can a moral principle be justified? Is there such a thing as moral truth? To do normative ethics, we must assume certain things about the meaning of moral terms and the logical relations among them. But the job of metaethics is to question all of these assumptions, to see if they really make sense.

Finally, there is **applied ethics**—the application of moral norms to specific moral issues or cases, particularly those in a profession such as medicine or law. Applied ethics in these fields goes under such names as medical ethics, journalistic ethics, and business ethics. In applied ethics we study the results derived from applying a moral principle or theory to specific circumstances. The purpose of the exercise is to learn something important about either the moral characteristics of the situation or the adequacy of the moral norms. Did the doctor do right in performing that abortion? Is it morally permissible for scientists to perform experiments on people without their consent? Was it right for the journalist to distort her reporting to aid a particular side in the war? Questions like these drive the search for answers in applied ethics.

In every division of ethics, we must be careful to distinguish between *values* and *obligations*. Sometimes we may be interested in concepts or judgments of *value*—that is, about what is morally *good, bad, blameworthy,* or *praiseworthy*. We properly use these kinds of terms to refer mostly to persons, character traits, motives, and intentions. We may say "She is a good person" or "He is to blame for that tragedy." Other times, we may be interested in concepts or judgments of *obligation*—that is, about what is obligatory or a duty, or what we should or ought to do. We use these terms to refer to *actions*. We may say "She has a duty to tell the truth" or "What he did was wrong."

When we talk about value in the sense just described, we mean *moral* value. If she is a good person, she is good in the moral sense. But we can also talk about *nonmoral* value. We can say that things such as televisions, rockets, experiences, and artwork (things other than persons and intentions) are good, but we mean "good" only in a nonmoral way. It makes no sense to assert that in themselves televisions or rockets are morally good or bad. Perhaps a rocket could be used to perform an action that is morally wrong. In that case, the action would be immoral, while the rocket itself would still have nonmoral value only.

Many things in life have value for us, but they are not necessarily valuable in the same way. Some things are valuable because they are a means to something else. We might say that gasoline is good because it is a means to make a gas-powered vehicle work, or that a pen is good because it can be used to write a letter. Such things are said to be **extrinsically valuable**—they are valuable as a means to something else. Some things, however, are valuable in themselves or for their own sakes. They are valuable simply because they are what they are, without being a means to something else. Things that have been regarded as valuable in themselves include happiness, pleasure, virtue, and beauty. These are said to be **intrinsically valuable**—they are valuable in themselves.

THE ELEMENTS OF ETHICS

We all do ethics, and we all have a general sense of what is involved. But we can still ask, What are the elements of ethics that make it the peculiar enterprise that it is? We can include at least the four factors described in this section.

The Preeminence of Reason

Doing ethics typically involves grappling with our feelings, taking into account the facts of the situation (including our own observations and relevant knowledge), and trying to understand the ideas that bear on the case. But above all, it involves, even requires, critical reasoning—the consideration of reasons for whatever statements (moral or otherwise) are in question. Whatever our view on moral issues and whatever moral outlook we subscribe to, our commonsense moral experience suggests that if a moral judgment is to be worthy of acceptance, it must be supported by good reasons, and our deliberations on the issue must include a consideration of those reasons.

The backbone of critical reasoning generally and moral reasoning in particular is logical argument. This kind of argument—not the angry-exchange type—consists of a statement to be supported (the assertion to be proved; the conclusion) and the statements that do the supporting (the reasons for believing the statement; the premises). With such arguments, we try to show that a moral judgment is or is not justified, that a moral principle is or is not sound, that an action is or is not morally permissible, or that a moral theory is or is not plausible.

Our use of critical reasoning and argument helps us keep our feelings about moral issues in perspective. Feelings are an important part of our moral experience. They make empathy possible, which gives us a deeper understanding of the human impact of moral norms. They also can serve as internal alarm bells, warning us of the possibility of injustice, suffering, and wrongdoing. But they are unreliable guides to moral truth. They may simply reflect our own emotional needs, prejudices, upbringing, culture, and self-interests. Careful reasoning, however, can inform our feelings and help us decide moral questions on their merits.

The Universal Perspective

Logic requires that moral norms and judgments follow the *principle of universalizability*—the idea that a moral statement (a principle, rule, or judgment) that applies in one situation must apply in all other situations that are relevantly similar. If you say, for example, that lying is wrong in a particular situation, then you implicitly agree that lying is wrong for anyone in relevantly similar situations. If you say that killing in self-defense is morally permissible, then you say in effect that killing in self-defense is permissible for everyone in relevantly similar situations.

It cannot be the case that an action performed by A is *wrong* while the same action performed by B in relevantly similar circumstances is *right*. It cannot be the case that the moral judgments formed in these two situations must differ just because two different people are involved.

This point about universalizability also applies to reasons used to support moral judgments. If reasons apply in a specific case, then those reasons also apply in all relevantly similar cases. It cannot be true that reasons that apply in a specific case do not apply to other cases that are similar in all relevant respects.

The Principle of Impartiality

From the moral point of view, all persons are considered equal and should be treated accordingly. This sense of impartiality is implied in all moral statements. It means that the welfare and interests of each individual should be given the same weight as all others. Unless there is a morally relevant difference between people, we should treat them the same: we must treat equals equally. We would think it outrageous for a moral rule to say something like "Everyone must refrain from stealing food in grocery stores—except for Mr. X, who may steal all he wants." Imagine that there is no morally relevant reason for making this exception to food stealing; Mr. X is exempted merely because, say, he is a celebrity known for outrageous behavior. We not only would object to this rule, we might even begin to wonder if it was a genuine moral rule at all because it lacks impartiality. Similarly, we would reject a moral rule that says something like "Everyone is entitled to basic human rights—except Native Americans." Such a rule would be a prime example of unfair discrimination based on race. We can see this blatant partiality best if we ask what morally relevant difference there is between Native Americans and everyone else. Differences in income, social status, skin color, ancestry, and the like are not morally relevant. Because there are no morally relevant differences, we must conclude that the rule sanctions unfair discrimination.

We must keep in mind, however, that sometimes there are good reasons for treating someone differently. Imagine a hospital that generally gives equal care to all patients, treating equals equally. Then suppose a patient comes to the hospital in an ambulance because she has had a heart attack and will die without immediate care. The hospital staff responds quickly, giving her faster and more sophisticated care than some other patients receive. Because the situation is a matter of life and death, it is a good reason for *not* treating everyone the same and for providing the heart attack patient with special consideration. This instance of discrimination is justified.

The Dominance of Moral Norms

Not all norms are moral norms. There are legal norms (laws, statutes), aesthetic norms (for judging artistic creations), prudential norms (practical considerations of self-interest), and others. Moral norms seem to stand out from all of these in an interesting way: they dominate. Whenever moral principles or values conflict in some way with nonmoral principles or values, the moral considerations usually override the others. Moral considerations seem more important, more critical, or more weighty. A principle of prudence such as "Never help a stranger" may be well justified, but it must yield to any moral principle that contradicts it, such as "Help a stranger in an emergency if you can do so without endangering yourself." An aesthetic norm that somehow involved violating a moral principle would have to take a backseat to the moral considerations. A law that conflicted with a moral principle would be suspect, and the latter would have to prevail over the former. Ultimately the justification for civil disobedience is that specific laws conflict with moral norms and are therefore invalid. If we judge a law to be bad, we usually do so on moral grounds.

RELIGION AND MORALITY

Many people believe that morality and religion are inseparable—that religion is the source or basis of morality and that moral precepts are simply what God says should be done. This view is not at all surprising because all religions imply or assert a perspective on morality. The three great religions in the Western tradition—Christianity, Judaism, and Islam—provide to their believers commandments or principles of conduct that are thought to constitute the moral law, the essence of morality. For millions of these adherents, the moral law is the will of God, and the will of God is the moral law. In the West at least, the powerful imprint of religion is evident in secular laws and in the private morality of believers and unbelievers alike. Secular systems of morality—for example, those of the ancient Greek philosophers, Immanuel Kant, the utilitarians, and others—have of course left their mark on Western ethics. But they have not moved the millions who think that morality is a product exclusively of religion.

So what is the relationship between religion and morality? For our purposes, we should break this question into two parts: (1) What is the relationship between religion and *ethics* (the philosophical study of morality), and (2) what is the relationship between religion and *morality* (beliefs about right and wrong)?

The first question asks how religion relates to the kind of investigation we conduct in this book—the use of experience and critical reasoning to study morality. The key point about the relationship is that whatever your views on religion and morality, an open-minded expedition into ethics is more useful and empowering than you may realize, especially now at the beginning of your journey into moral philosophy. You may believe, for example, that God determines what is right and wrong, so there is no need to apply critical reasoning to morality—you just need to know what God says. But this judgment—and similar dismissals of ethics—would be premature.

Believers Need Moral Reasoning

It is difficult—perhaps impossible—for most people to avoid using moral reasoning. Religious people are no exception. One reason is that religious moral codes (such as the Ten Commandments) and other major religious rules of conduct are usually vague, laying out general principles that may be difficult to apply to specific cases. (Secular moral codes, such as the "Golden Rule," often have the same disadvantage.) For example, we may be commanded to love our neighbor, but who are our neighbors? Do they include people of a different religion? people who denounce our religion? the gay or lesbian couple? those who steal from us? the convicted child molester next door? the drug dealers on the corner? the woman who got an abortion? Also, what does loving our neighbor demand of us? How does love require us to behave toward the drug dealers, the gay couple, or the person who denounces our religion? If our terminally ill neighbor asks us in the name of love to help him kill himself, what should we do? Does love require us to kill him—or to refrain from killing him? And, of course, commandments can conflict—as when, for example, the only way to avoid killing an innocent person is to tell a lie, or the only way to save the life of one person is to kill another. All of these situations force the believer to interpret religious directives, to try to apply general rules to specific cases, and to draw out the implications of particular views—in other words, to do ethics.

When Conflicts Arise, Ethics Steps In

Very often moral contradictions or inconsistencies confront the religious believer, and only moral reasoning can help resolve them. Believers sometimes disagree with their religious leaders on moral issues. Adherents of one religious tradition may disagree with those from another tradition on whether an act is right or wrong. Sincere devotees in a religious tradition may wonder if its moral teachings make sense. In all such cases, intelligent resolution of the conflict of moral claims can be achieved only by applying a neutral standard that helps sort out the competing viewpoints. Moral philosophy supplies the neutral standard in the form of critical thinking, well-made arguments, and careful analysis. No wonder then that many great religious minds—Aquinas, Leibniz, Descartes, Kant, Maimonides, Averroës, and others—have relied on reason to examine the nature of morality. In fact, countless theists have regarded reason as a gift from God that enables human beings to grasp the truths of science, life, and morality.

Moral Philosophy Enables Productive Discourse

Any fruitful discussions about morality undertaken between people from different religious traditions or between believers and nonbelievers will require a common set of ethical concepts and a shared procedure for deciding issues and making judgments. Ethics provides these tools. Without them, conversations will resolve nothing, and participants will learn little. Without them, people will talk past each other, appealing only to their own religious views. Furthermore, in a pluralistic society, most of the public discussions about important moral issues take place in a context of shared values such as justice, fairness, equality, and tolerance. Just as important, they also occur according to an unwritten understanding that (1) moral positions should be explained, (2) claims should be supported by reasons, and (3) reasoning should be judged by common rational standards. These skills, of course, are at the heart of ethics.

Now consider the second question from above: What is the relationship between religion and morality? For many people, the most interesting query about the relationship between religion and morality is this: Is God the maker of morality? That is, is God the author of the moral law? Those who answer yes are endorsing a theory of morality known as the **divine command theory**. It says that right actions are those that are willed by God, that God literally defines right and wrong. Something is right or good only because God makes it so. In the simplest version of the theory, God can determine right and wrong because he is omnipotent. He is all-powerful—powerful enough even to create moral norms. In this view, God is a divine lawgiver, and his laws constitute morality.

In general, believers are divided on whether the divine command theory gives an accurate account of the source of morality. Notable among the theory's detractors are the great theistic philosophers Gottfried Leibniz (1646–1716) and Thomas Aquinas (1225–1274). And conversely, as odd as it may sound, some nonbelievers have subscribed to it. In Fyodor Dostoyevsky's novel *The Brothers Karamazov* (1879–80), the character Ivan Karamazov declares, "If God doesn't exist, everything is permissible." This very sentiment was espoused by, among others, the famous atheist philosopher Jean-Paul Sartre.

Both religious and secular critics of the divine command theory believe that it poses a serious dilemma, one first articulated by Socrates two and a half millennia ago. In the dialogue *Euthyphro*, Socrates asks, Is an action morally right because God wills it to be so, or does God will it to be so because it is morally right? Critics say that if an action is right only because God wills it (that is, if right and wrong are dependent on God), then many heinous crimes and evil actions would be right if God willed them. If God willed murder, theft, or torture, these deeds would be morally right. If God has unlimited power, he could easily will such actions. If the rightness of an action depended on God's will alone, he could not have reasons for willing what he wills. No reasons would be available and none required. Therefore, if God commanded an action, the command would be without reason, completely arbitrary.

Neither the believer nor the nonbeliever would think this state of affairs plausible. On the other hand, if God wills an action because it is morally right (if moral norms are independent of God), then the divine command theory must be false. God does not create rightness; he simply knows what is right and wrong and is subject to the moral law just as humans are.

For some theists, this charge of arbitrariness is especially worrisome. Leibniz, for example, rejects the divine command theory, declaring that it implies that God is unworthy of worship:

> In saying, therefore, that things are not good according to any
> standard of goodness, but simply by the will of God, it seems
> to me that one destroys, without realizing it, all the love of God
> and all his glory; for why praise him for what he has done, if he
> would be equally praiseworthy in doing the contrary? Where will
> be his justice and his wisdom if he has only a certain despotic
> power, if arbitrary will takes the place of reasonableness, and if in
> accord with the definition of tyrants, justice consists in that which
> is pleasing to the most powerful?[3]

Defenders of the divine command theory may reply to the arbitrariness argument by contending that God would never command us to commit heinous acts, because God is all good. Because of his supreme goodness, he would will only what is good. Some thinkers, however, believe that such reasoning renders the very idea of God's goodness meaningless. As one philosopher says,

> [O]n this view, the doctrine of the goodness of God is reduced
> to nonsense. It is important to religious believers that God is not
> only all-powerful and all-knowing, but that he is also good; yet if
> we accept the idea that good and bad are defined by reference to
> God's will, this notion is deprived of any meaning. What could it
> mean to say that God's commands are good? If "X is good" means
> "X is commanded by God," then "God's commands are good"
> would mean only "God's commands are commanded by God," an
> empty truism.[4]

In any case, it seems that through critical reasoning we can indeed learn much about morality and the moral life. After all, there are complete moral systems (some of which are examined in this book) that are not based on religion, that contain genuine moral norms indistinguishable from those embraced by religion, and that are justified not by reference to religious precepts but by careful thinking and moral arguments. Moreover, if we can do ethics—if we can use critical reasoning to discern moral norms certified by the best reasons and evidence—then critical reasoning is sufficient to guide us to moral standards and values. Because we obviously can do ethics (as the following chapters demonstrate), morality is both accessible and meaningful to us whether we are religious or not.

KEYWORDS

applied ethics—The application of moral norms to specific moral issues or cases, particularly those in a profession such as medicine or law.

descriptive ethics—The scientific study of moral beliefs and practices.

divine command theory—A theory asserting that the morally right action is the one that God commands.

ethics (or *moral philosophy*)—The philosophical study of morality.

extrinsically valuable—Valuable as a means to something else, such as the pen that can be used to write a letter.

intrinsically valuable—Valuable in itself, for its own sake, such as happiness or beauty.

metaethics—The study of the meaning and logical structure of moral beliefs.

morality—Beliefs concerning right and wrong, good and bad; they can include judgments, rules, principles, and theories.

normative ethics—The study of the principles, rules, or theories that guide our actions and judgments.

EXERCISES

Review Questions

1. When can it be said that your moral beliefs are not really yours?
2. In what ways are we forced to do ethics? What is at stake in these deliberations?
3. What is the unfortunate result of accepting moral beliefs without questioning them?
4. Can our feelings be our sole guide to morality? Why or why not?
5. What are some questions asked in normative ethics?
6. What is the difference between normative ethics and metaethics?
7. What is the dilemma about God and morality posed by Socrates in *Euthyphro*?
8. What kinds of moral contradictions or inconsistencies confront religious believers?
9. What are the premises in the arbitrariness argument against the divine command theory?
10. Does the principle of impartiality imply that we must always treat equals equally?

Essay Questions

1. Give an example of how you or someone you know has used reasons to support a moral judgment.
2. Provide examples of moral beliefs that you have absorbed or adopted without question.
3. Identify at least two important normative ethical questions that you have wondered about in the past year.
4. Cite an example of how the principle of universalizability has entered into your moral deliberations.
5. How does racial discrimination violate the principle of impartiality?
6. Do you think that morality ultimately depends on God (that God is the author of the moral law)? Why or why not?
7. How could the divine command theory undermine any reasons we might have for respecting God?
8. Explain how some believers respond to the arbitrariness problem in the divine command theory. Is their response plausible? Why or why not?

ETHICAL DILEMMAS

1. You are the mayor of a major city, and you want to keep the streets as clean as possible. You send the city's street sweepers to the more affluent neighborhoods, but you ignore the poorer neighborhoods because the poor residents pay less in taxes than the rich people do. Is this practice a violation of the impartiality principle? Why or why not?
2. You try to live strictly by the moral rules contained in your religion's moral code. The two most important rules are "Be merciful" (don't give people what they deserve) and "Be just" (give people exactly what they deserve). Now suppose a man is arrested for stealing food from your house, and the police leave it up to you whether he should be prosecuted for his crime or set free. Should you be merciful and set him free, or be just and make sure he is appropriately punished? How do you resolve this conflict of rules? Can your moral code resolve it? To what moral principles or theories do you appeal?
3. Suppose you are an engineer building a road across a mountain. From a prudential point of view, it would be easier and cheaper to build it through a family's farm. This option would require compelling the

family to move, which would be an extreme hardship for them. From a moral point of view, the family should be allowed to stay on their farm. Which view should take precedence?

Endnotes

1. John Stuart Mill, *On Liberty*, 1859.
2. Paul W. Taylor, *Principles of Ethics: An Introduction* (Encino, CA: Dickenson, 1975), 9–10.
3. G. W. von Leibniz, "Discourse on Metaphysics," in *Selections*, ed. Philip P. Wiener (New York: Scribner, 1951), 292.
4. James Rachels, *The Elements of Moral Philosophy,* 4th ed. (Boston: McGraw-Hill, 2003), 51.

CHAPTER 2

Relativism and Emotivism

Consider the following: Abdulla Yones killed his sixteen-year-old daughter Heshu in their apartment in west London. The murder was yet another example of an "honor killing," an ancient tradition still practiced in many parts of the world. Using a kitchen knife, Yones stabbed Heshu eleven times and slit her throat. He later declared that he *had* to kill her to expunge a stain from his family, a stain that Heshu had caused by her outrageous behavior. What was outrageous behavior to Yones, however, would seem to many Westerners to be typical teenage antics, annoying but benign. Heshu's precise offense against her family's honor is unclear, but the possibilities include wearing makeup, having a boyfriend, and showing an independent streak that would be thought perfectly normal throughout the West. In some countries, honor killings are sometimes endorsed by the local community or even given the tacit blessing of the state.

What do you think of this time-honored way of dealing with family conflicts? Specifically, what is your opinion regarding the *morality* of honor killing? Your response to this question is likely to reveal not only your view of honor killing but your overall approach to morality as well. Suppose your response is something like this: "Honor killing is morally *wrong*—wrong no matter where it's done or who does it." With this statement, you implicitly embrace moral **objectivism**, the doctrine that some moral norms or principles are valid for everyone—*universal*, in other words—regardless of how cultures may differ in their moral outlooks. You need not hold, however, that the objective principles are rigid rules with no exceptions (a view known as *absolutism*) or that they must be applied in exactly the same way in every situation and culture.

On the other hand, let us say that you assess the case like this: "In societies that approve of honor killing, the practice is morally right; in those that do not approve, it is morally wrong. My society approves of honor killing, so it is morally right." If you believe what you say, then you are a cultural relativist. **Cultural relativism** is the view that an action is morally right if one's culture approves of it. Moral rightness and wrongness are therefore relative to cultures. So in one culture, an action may be morally right; in another culture, it may be morally wrong.

Perhaps you prefer an even narrower view of morality, and so you say, "Honor killing may be right for you, but it is most certainly not right for me." If you mean this literally, then you are committed to another kind of relativism called **subjective relativism**—the view that an action is morally right if one approves of it. Moral rightness and wrongness are relative not to cultures but to individuals. An action then can be right for you but wrong for someone else. Your approving of an action makes it right. There is therefore no objective morality, and cultural norms do not make right or wrong—individuals make right or wrong.

Finally, imagine that you wish to take a different tack regarding the subject of honor killing. You say, "I abhor the practice of honor killing," but you believe that in uttering these words you are saying nothing that is true or false. You believe that despite what your statement seems to mean, you are simply expressing your emotions. You therefore hold to **emotivism**—the view that moral utterances are neither true nor false but are instead expressions of emotions or attitudes. So in your sentence about honor killing, you are not stating a fact—you are merely emoting and possibly trying to influence someone's behavior. Even when emotivists express a more specific preference regarding other people's behavior—by saying, for instance, "No one should commit an honor killing"—they are still not making a factual claim. They are simply expressing a preference, and perhaps hoping to persuade other people to see things their way.

These four replies represent four distinctive perspectives (though certainly not the only perspectives) on the meaning and import of moral judgments. Moreover, they are not purely theoretical but real and relevant. People actually live their lives (or try to) as moral objectivists or relativists, or some strange and inconsistent mixture of these. (There is an excellent chance, for example, that you were raised as an objectivist but now accept some form of relativism, or that you even try to hold to objectivism in some instances and relativism in others.)

In any case, the question that you should ask—and that moral philosophy can help you answer—is not whether you in fact accept any of these views, but whether you are justified in doing so. Let us see, then, where an examination of reasons for and against them will lead.

SUBJECTIVE RELATIVISM

What view of morality could be more tempting (and convenient) than the notion that an action is right if someone approves of it? Subjective relativism says that action X is right for Ann if she approves of it yet wrong for Greg if he disapproves of it. Thus action X can be both right and wrong—right for Ann but wrong for Greg. A person's approval of an action *makes it right* for that person. Action X is not *objectively* right (or wrong). It is right (or wrong) relative to individuals. In this way, moral rightness becomes a matter of personal taste. If Ann thinks strawberry ice cream tastes good, then it is good (for her). If Greg thinks strawberry ice cream tastes bad, then it is bad (for him). There is no such thing as strawberry ice cream tasting good objectively or generally. Likewise, the morality of an action depends on Ann and Greg's moral tastes.

Many people claim they are subjective relativists, until they realize the implications of the doctrine—implications that are at odds with our commonsense moral experience. First, subjective relativism implies that in the rendering of any moral opinion, each person is incapable of being in error. Each of us is *morally infallible*. If we approve of an action—and we are sincere in our approval—then that action is morally right. We literally cannot be mistaken about this, because our approval makes the action right. If we say that inflicting pain on an innocent child for no reason is right (that is, we approve of such an action), then the action is right. Our moral judgment is correct, and it cannot be otherwise. Yet if anything is obvious about our moral experience, it is that we are *not* infallible. We sometimes *are* mistaken in our moral judgments. We are, after all, not gods.

From all accounts, Adolf Hitler approved of (and ordered) the extermination of vast numbers of innocent people, including six million Jews. If so, by the lights of subjective relativism, his facilitating those deaths was morally right. It seems that the totalitarian leader Pol Pot approved of his murdering more than a million innocent people in Cambodia. If so, it was right for him to murder those people. But it seems obvious that what these men did was wrong, and their approving of their own actions did not make the actions right. Because subjective relativism suggests otherwise, it is a dubious doctrine.

Another obvious feature of our commonsense moral experience is that from time to time we have moral disagreements. Maria says that capital punishment is right, but Carlos says that it is wrong. This seems like a perfectly clear case of two people disagreeing about the morality of capital punishment. Subjective relativism, however, implies that such disagreements cannot happen. Subjective relativism says that when Maria states that capital punishment is right, she is just saying that she approves of it. And when Carlos states that capital punishment is wrong, he is just saying that he disapproves of it. They are not really disagreeing, merely describing their attitudes toward capital punishment. In effect, Maria is saying "This is my attitude on the subject," and Carlos is saying "Here is my attitude on the subject." These two claims are not opposed to one another, because they are about different subjects. So both statements could be true. Maria and Carlos might as well be discussing how strawberry ice cream tastes to each of them, for nothing that Maria says could contradict what Carlos says. However, because genuine disagreement is a fact of our moral life, and subjective relativism is inconsistent with this fact, the doctrine is implausible.

In practice, subjective relativism is a difficult view to hold consistently. At times, of course, you can insist that an action is right for you but wrong for someone else. But you may also find yourself saying something like "Pol Pot committed absolutely heinous acts; he was evil" or "What Hitler did was wrong"—and what you mean is that what Pol Pot and Hitler did was objectively wrong, not just wrong relative to you. Such slides from subjective relativism to objectivism suggest a conflict between these two perspectives and the need to resolve it through critical reasoning.

CULTURAL RELATIVISM

To many people, the idea that morality is relative to culture is obvious. It seems obvious primarily because modern sociology has left no doubt that people's moral judgments differ from culture to culture.

The moral judgments of people in other cultures are often shockingly different from our own. In some societies, it is morally permissible to kill infants at birth, burn widows alive with the bodies of their husbands, steal and commit acts of treachery, surgically remove the clitorises of young girls for no medical reason, kill one's elderly parents, have multiple husbands or wives, and make up for someone's death by murdering others. Among some people, it has been considered morally acceptable to kill those of a different sexual orientation, lynch persons with a different skin color, and allow children to die by refusing to give them available medical treatment. (These latter acts have all been practiced in subcultures within the United States, so not all such cultural differences happen far from home.) There is only a small step from acknowledging this moral diversity among cultures to the conclusion that cultures determine moral rightness and that objective morality is a myth.

The philosopher Walter T. Stace (1886–1967) illustrates how easily this conclusion has come to many in Western societies:

> It was easy enough to believe in a single absolute morality in older times when there was no anthropology, when all humanity was divided clearly into two groups, Christian peoples and the "heathen." Christian peoples knew and possessed the one true morality. The rest were savages whose moral ideas could be ignored. But all this changed. Greater knowledge has brought greater tolerance. We can no longer exalt our own moralities as alone true, while dismissing all other moralities as false or inferior. The investigations of anthropologists have shown that there exist side by side in the world a bewildering variety of moral codes. On this topic endless volumes have been written, masses of evidence piled up. Anthropologists have ransacked the Melanesian Islands, the jungles of New Guinea, the steppes of Siberia, the deserts of Australia, the forests of central Africa, and have brought back with them countless examples of weird, extravagant, and fantastic "moral" customs with which to confound us. We learn that all kinds of horrible practices are, in this, that, or the other place, regarded as essential to virtue. We find that there is nothing, or next to nothing, which has always and everywhere been regarded as morally good by all men. Where then is our universal morality? Can we, in face of all this evidence, deny that it is nothing but an empty dream?[1]

Here, Stace spells out in rough form the most common argument for cultural relativism, an inference from differences in the moral beliefs of cultures to the conclusion that cultures make morality. Before we conclude that objectivism is in fact an empty dream, we should state the argument more precisely and examine it closely. We can lay out the argument like this:

1. People's judgments about right and wrong differ from culture to culture.

2. If people's judgments about right and wrong differ from culture to culture, then right and wrong are relative to culture, and there are no objective moral principles.

3. Therefore, right and wrong are relative to culture, and there are no objective moral principles.

A good argument gives us good reason to accept its conclusion. An argument is good if its logic is solid (the conclusion follows logically from the premises) *and* the premises are true. So is the foregoing argument a good one? We can see right away that the logic is in fact solid. That is, the argument is valid: the conclusion does indeed follow from the premises. The question then becomes whether the premises are true. As we have seen, Premise 1 is most certainly true. People's judgments about right and wrong do vary from culture to culture. But what of Premise 2? Does the diversity of views about right and wrong among cultures show that right and wrong are determined by culture, that there are no universal moral truths? There are good reasons to think this premise false.

Premise 2 says that because there are disagreements among cultures about right and wrong, there must not be any universal standards of right and wrong. But even if the moral judgments of people in various cultures do differ, such difference in itself does not show that morality is relative to culture. Just because people in different cultures have different views about morality, their disagreement does not prove that no view can be objectively correct—no more than people's disagreements about the size of a house show that no one's opinion about it can be objectively true. Suppose culture A endorses infanticide, but culture B does not. Such a disagreement does not demonstrate that both cultures are equally correct or that there is no objectively correct answer. After all, it is possible that infanticide is objectively right (or wrong) and that the relevant moral beliefs of either culture A or culture B are false.

Another reason to doubt the truth of Premise 2 comes from questioning how deep the disagreements among cultures really are. Judgments about the rightness of actions obviously do vary across cultures. But people can differ in their moral judgments not just because they accept different moral principles, but also because they have divergent *nonmoral* beliefs. They may actually embrace the *same* moral principles, but their moral judgments conflict because their nonmoral beliefs lead them to apply those principles in very different ways. If so, the diversity of moral judgments across cultures does not necessarily indicate deep disagreements over fundamental moral principles or standards. Here is a classic example:

> [T]he story is told of a culture in which a son is regarded as obligated to kill his father when the latter reaches age sixty. Given just this much information about the culture and the practice in question it is tempting to conclude that the members of that culture differ radically from members of our culture in their moral beliefs and attitudes. We, after all, believe it is immoral to take a human life, and regard patricide as especially wrong. But suppose that in the culture we are considering, those who belong to it believe (a) that at the moment of death one enters heaven; (b) one's physical and mental condition in the afterlife is exactly what it is at the moment of death; and (c) men are at the peak of their physical and mental powers when they are sixty. Then what appeared at first to be peculiarities in moral outlook on the part of the cultural group in question regarding the sanctity of life and respect for parents, turn out to be located rather in a nonmoral outlook of the group. A man in that culture who kills his father is doing so out of concern for the latter's well-being—to prevent him, for example, from spending eternity blind or senile. It is not at all clear that, if we shared the relevant nonmoral beliefs of this other culture, we would not believe with them that sons should kill their fathers at the appropriate time.[2]

To find similar examples, we need not search for the exotic. In Western cultures we have the familiar case of abortion, an issue hotly debated among those who at first glance appear to be disagreeing about moral principles. But in fact the disputants agree about the moral principle involved: that murder (unjustly killing a person) is morally wrong. What they do disagree about is a nonmoral factual matter—whether the fetus is an entity that can be murdered (that is, whether it is a person). Disagreement over the nonmoral facts masks substantial agreement on fundamental moral standards.

The work of several anthropologists provides some evidence for these kinds of disagreements, as well as for the existence of cross-cultural moral agreement in general. The social psychologist Solomon Asch, for instance, maintains that differing moral judgments among societies often arise when the same moral principles are operating but the particulars of cultural situations vary.[3] Other observers claim that across numerous diverse cultures we can find many common moral elements, such as prohibitions against murder, lying, incest, and adultery and obligations of fairness, reciprocity, and consideration toward parents and children.[4] Some philosophers argue that a core set of moral values—including, for example, truth telling and prohibitions against murder—must be universal, otherwise cultures would not survive.

These points demonstrate that Premise 2 of the argument for cultural relativism is false. The argument therefore gives us no good reasons to believe that an action is right simply because one's culture approves of it.

For many people, however, the failure of the argument for cultural relativism may be beside the point. They find the doctrine appealing mainly because it seems to promote the humane and enlightened attitude of tolerance toward other cultures. Broad expanses of history are drenched with blood and marked by cruelty because of the evil of intolerance—religious, racial, political, and social. Tolerance therefore seems a supreme virtue, and cultural relativism appears to provide a justification and vehicle for it. After all, if all cultures are morally equal, does not cultural relativism both entail and promote tolerance?

We should hope that tolerance does reign in a pluralistic world, but there is no necessary connection between tolerance and cultural relativism. For one thing, cultural relativists cannot consistently advocate tolerance. To advocate tolerance is to advocate an objective moral value. But if tolerance is an objective moral value, then cultural relativism must be false, because it says that there are no objective moral values. So instead of justifying tolerance toward all, cultural relativism actually undercuts universal tolerance. Moreover, according to cultural relativism, intolerance can be justified just as easily as tolerance can. If a culture approves of intolerance, then intolerance is right for that culture. If a culture approves of tolerance, then tolerance is right for that culture. Cultural relativists are thus committed to the view that intolerance can in fact be justified, and they cannot consistently claim that tolerance is morally right everywhere.

At this point we are left with no good reasons to believe that cultural relativism is true. But the problems for the doctrine go deeper than this. Like subjective relativism, cultural relativism has several implications that render it highly implausible.

First, as is the case with subjective relativism, cultural relativism implies moral infallibility. A culture simply cannot be mistaken about a moral issue. If it approves of an action, then that action is morally right, and there is no possibility of error as long as the culture's approval is genuine. But, of course, cultural infallibility in moral matters is flagrantly implausible, just as individual infallibility is. At one time or another, cultures have sanctioned witch burning, slavery, genocide, racism, rape, human sacrifice, and religious persecution. Does it make any sense to say that they could not have been mistaken about the morality of these actions?

Cultural relativism also has the peculiar consequence that social reformers of every sort would *always be wrong*. Their culture would be the ultimate authority on moral matters, so if they disagree with their culture, they could not possibly be right. If their culture approves of genocide, then genocide would be right, and anti-genocide reformers would be wrong to oppose the practice. In this upside-down world, the anti-genocide reformers would be immoral and the genocidal culture would be the real paragon of righteousness. Reformers such as Martin Luther King Jr., Mahatma Gandhi, Mary Wollstonecraft (champion of women's rights), and Frederick Douglass (American abolitionist) would be great crusaders—for immorality. Our moral experience, however, suggests that cultural relativism has matters exactly backward. Social reformers have often been right when they claimed their cultures were wrong, and this fact suggests that cultural relativism is wrong about morality.

Wherever cultural relativism holds, if you have a disagreement with your culture about the rightness of an action, you automatically lose. You are in error by definition. But what about a disagreement among members of the same society? What would such a disagreement amount to? It amounts to something very strange, according to cultural relativism. When two people in the same culture disagree on a moral issue, what they are really disagreeing about—the only thing they can rationally disagree about—is whether their society endorses a particular view. After all, society makes actions right by approving or disapproving of them. According to cultural relativism, if René and Michel (both members of society X) are disagreeing about capital punishment, their disagreement must actually be about whether society X approves of capital punishment. Because right and wrong are determined by one's culture, René and Michel are disagreeing about what society X says. But this view of moral disagreement is dubious, to say the least. When we have a moral disagreement, we do not think that the crux of it is whether our society approves of an action. We do not think that deciding a moral issue is simply a matter of polling the public to see which way opinion leans. We do not think that René and Michel will ever find out whether capital punishment is morally permissible by consulting public opinion. Determining whether an action is right is a very different thing from determining what most people think. This odd consequence of cultural relativism suggests that the doctrine is flawed.

One of the more disturbing implications of cultural relativism is that cultures cannot be legitimately criticized from the outside. If a culture approves of the actions that it performs, then those actions are morally right regardless of what other cultures have to say about the matter. One society's practices are as morally justified as any other's, as long as the practices are socially sanctioned. This consequence of cultural relativism may not seem too worrisome when the societies in question are long dead. But it takes on a different tone when the societies are closer to us in time. Consider the 1994 genocide committed in Rwanda in which nearly a million people died. Suppose the killers' society (their tribe) approved of the murders. Then the genocide was morally justified. If you are a cultural relativist, you cannot legitimately condemn these monstrous deeds. Because they were approved by their respective societies, they were morally justified. They were just as morally justified as the socially sanctioned and life-saving activities of Albert Schweitzer, Jonas Salk, or Florence Nightingale. But all of this seems implausible. We do in fact sometimes criticize other cultures and believe that it is legitimate to do so.

Contrary to the popular view, rejecting cultural relativism (embracing moral objectivism) does not entail intolerance. In fact, it provides a plausible starting point for tolerance. A moral objectivist realizes that she can legitimately criticize other cultures, and that people of other cultures can legitimately criticize her culture. A recognition of this fact, together with an objectivist's sense of fallibility, can lead her to an openness to criticism of her own culture and to acceptance of everyone's right to disagree.

We not only criticize other cultures, but we also compare the past with the present. We compare the actions of the past with those of the present and judge whether moral progress has been made. We see that slavery has been abolished, that we no longer burn witches, that we recognize racism as evil, and then we judge that these changes represent moral progress. For moral relativists, however, there is no objective standard by which to compare the ways of the past with the ways of the present. Societies of the past approved or disapproved of certain practices, and contemporary societies approve or disapprove of them, and no transcultural moral assessments can be made. But if there is such a thing as moral progress, then there must be some cross-cultural moral yardstick by which we can evaluate actions. There must be objective standards by which we can judge that the actions of the present are better than those of the past. If there are no objective moral standards, our judging that we are in fact making moral progress is hard to explain.

Finally, there is a fundamental difficulty concerning the application of cultural relativism to moral questions: the doctrine is nearly impossible to use. The problem is that cultural relativism applies to societies (or social groups), but we all belong to several societies, and there is no way to choose which one is the proper one. What society do you belong to if you are an Italian American Buddhist living in Atlanta, Georgia, who is a member of the National Organization for Women and a breast cancer support group? The hope of cultural relativists is that they can use the doctrine to make better, more enlightened moral decisions. But this society-identification problem seems to preclude any moral decisions, let alone enlightened ones.

What, then, can we conclude from our examination of cultural relativism? We have found that the basic argument for the view fails; we therefore have no good reasons to believe that the doctrine is true. Beyond that, we have good grounds for thinking the doctrine false. Its surprising implications regarding moral infallibility, moral reformers, moral progress, the nature of moral disagreements within societies, and the possibility of cross-cultural criticism show it to be highly implausible. The crux of the matter is that cultural relativism does a poor job of explaining some important features of our moral experience. A far better explanation of these features is that some form of moral objectivism is true.

EMOTIVISM

The commonsense view of moral judgments is that they ascribe moral properties to such things as actions and people and that they are therefore statements that can be true or false. This view of moral judgments is known as *cognitivism*. The opposing view, called *noncognitivism*, denies that moral judgments are statements that can be true or false; rather, moral judgments do not ascribe properties to anything. Probably the most famous noncognitivist view is emotivism, which says that moral judgments cannot be true or false because they do not make any claims—they merely express emotions or attitudes. For the emotivist, moral utterances are something akin to exclamations that simply express approving or disapproving feelings: "Violence against women—disgusting!" or "Shoplifting—love it!"

The English philosopher A. J. Ayer (1910–1989), an early champion of emotivism, is clear and blunt about what a moral utterance such as "Stealing money is wrong" signifies. This sentence, he says,

> expresses no proposition which can be either true or false. It is as if I had written "Stealing money!!"—where the shape and thickness of the exclamation marks show, by a suitable convention, that a special sort of moral disapproval is the feeling which is being expressed. It is clear that there is nothing said here which can be true or false. . . . For in saying that a certain type of action is right or wrong, I am not making any factual statement, not even a statement about my own state of mind.[5]

If moral judgments are about feelings and not the truth or falsity of moral assertions, then ethics is a very different sort of inquiry than most people imagine. As Ayer says,

> [A]s ethical judgments are mere expressions of feeling, there can be no way of determining the validity of any ethical system, and, indeed, no sense in asking whether any such system is true. All that

one may legitimately enquire in this connection is, What are the moral habits of a given person or group of people, and what causes them to have precisely those habits and feelings? And this enquiry falls wholly within the scope of the existing social sciences.[6]

The emotivist points out that although moral utterances express feelings and attitudes, they also function to influence people's attitudes and behavior. So the sentence "Stealing money is wrong" not only expresses feelings of disapproval, it also can influence others to have similar feelings and act accordingly.

Emotivists also take an unusual position on moral disagreements. They maintain that moral disagreements are not conflicts of beliefs, as is the case when one person asserts that something is the case and another person asserts that it is not the case. Instead, moral disagreements are *disagreements in attitude.* Jane has positive feelings or a favorable attitude toward abortion, but Ellen has negative feelings or an unfavorable attitude toward abortion. The disagreement is emotive, not cognitive. Jane may say "Abortion is right," and Ellen may say "Abortion is wrong," but they are not really disagreeing over the facts. They are expressing conflicting attitudes and trying to influence each other's attitude and behavior.

Philosophers have criticized emotivism on several grounds, and this emotivist analysis of disagreement has been a prime target. As you might suspect, the concern is that this notion of disagreement is radically different from our ordinary view. Like subjective relativism, emotivism implies that disagreements in the usual sense are impossible. People cannot disagree over the moral facts, because there are no moral facts. But we tend to think that when we disagree with someone on a moral issue, there really is a conflict of statements about what is the case. Of course, when we are involved in a conflict of beliefs, we may also experience conflicting attitudes. But we do not think that we are *only* experiencing a disagreement in attitudes.

Emotivism also provides a curious account of how reasons function in moral discourse. Our commonsense view is that a moral judgment is the kind of thing that makes a claim about moral properties and that such a claim can be supported by reasons. If someone asserts "Euthanasia is wrong," we may sensibly ask him what reasons he has for believing this claim. If he replies that there are no reasons to back up his claim or that moral utterances are not the kind of things that can be supported by reasons, we would probably think that he misunderstood the question or the nature of morality. For the emotivist, "moral" reasons have a very different function. They are intended not to support statements (since there are no moral statements) but to influence the emotions or attitudes of others. Because moral utterances express emotions or attitudes, "presenting reasons" is a matter of offering nonmoral facts that can influence those emotions and attitudes. Suppose A has a favorable attitude toward abortion, and B has an unfavorable one (that is, A and B are having a disagreement in attitude). For A, to present reasons is to provide information that might cause B to have a more favorable attitude toward abortion.

This conception of the function of reasons, however, implies that good reasons can encompass *any* nonmoral facts that alter someone's attitude. In this view, the relevance of these facts to the judgment at hand is beside the point. The essential criterion is whether the adduced facts are sufficiently influential. They need not have any logical or cognitive connection to the moral judgment to be changed. They may, for example, appeal to someone's ignorance, arrogance, racism, or fear. But we ordinarily suppose that reasons *should* be relevant to the cognitive content of moral judgments. Moreover, we normally make a clear distinction between influencing someone's attitudes and showing (by providing relevant reasons) that a claim is true—a distinction that emotivism cannot make.

The final implication of emotivism—that there is no such thing as goodness or badness—is also problematic. We cannot legitimately claim that anything is good or bad, because these properties do not exist. To declare that something is good is just to express positive emotions or a favorable attitude toward it. We may say that pain is bad, but badness (or goodness) is not a feature of pain. Our saying that pain is bad is just an expression of our unfavorable attitude toward pain.

Suppose a six-year-old girl is living in a small village in Syria during the civil war between President Bashar al-Assad's Baathist government and rebel forces. Assad's henchmen firebomb the village, destroying it and incinerating everyone except the girl, who is burned from head to toe and endures excruciating pain for three days before she dies. Suppose that we are deeply moved by this tragedy as we consider her unimaginable suffering and we remark, "How horrible. The little girl's suffering was a very bad thing."[7] When we say something like this, we ordinarily mean that the girl's suffering had a certain moral property:

that the suffering was bad. But according to emotivism, her suffering had no moral properties at all. When we comment on the girl's suffering, we are simply expressing our feelings; the suffering itself was neither good nor bad. But this view of things seems implausible. Our moral experience suggests that in fact some things are bad and some are good.

The philosopher Brand Blanshard (1892–1987) makes the point this way:

> [T]he emotivist is cut off by his theory from admitting that there has been anything good or evil in the past, either animal or human. There have been Black Deaths, to be sure, and wars and rumours of war; there have been the burning of countless women as witches, and the massacre in the Katlyn forest, and Oswiecim, and Dachau, and an unbearable procession of horrors; but one cannot meaningfully say that anything evil has ever happened. The people who suffered from these things did indeed take up attitudes of revulsion toward them; we can now judge that they took them; but in such judgments we are not saying that anything evil occurred. . . . [Emotivism], when first presented, has some plausibility. But when this is balanced against the implied unplausibility of setting down as meaningless every suggestion that good or evil events have ever occurred, it is outweighed enormously.[8]

Obviously, emotivism does not fare well when examined in light of our commonsense moral experience. We must keep in mind, though, that common sense is fallible. On the other hand, we should not jettison common sense in favor of another view unless we have good reasons to do so. In the case of emotivism, we have no good reasons to prefer it over common sense—and we have good grounds for rejecting it.

KEYWORDS

cultural relativism—The view that an action is morally right if one's culture approves of it.

emotivism—The view that moral utterances are neither true nor false but are expressions of emotions or attitudes.

objectivism—The view that some moral principles are valid for everyone.

subjective relativism—The view that an action is morally right if one approves of it.

EXERCISES

Review Questions

1. Does objectivism entail intolerance?
2. Does objectivism require absolutism?
3. How does subjective relativism differ from cultural relativism?
4. How does subjective relativism imply moral infallibility?
5. How does subjective relativism imply that disagreements cannot happen?
6. What is the argument for cultural relativism? Is it a valid argument?
7. Can cultural relativists consistently advocate tolerance? Why or why not?
8. What is the emotivist view of moral disagreements?
9. According to emotivism, how do reasons function in moral discourse?
10. Does the diversity of moral judgments in cultures show that right and wrong are determined by culture? Why or why not?

Essay Questions

1. Are you a subjective relativist? If so, what are your reasons for adopting this view? If not, why not?
2. Suppose a majority of the German people approved of Hitler's murdering six million Jews in World War II. Would this approval make Hitler's actions morally justified? If so, why? If not, why not—and what moral outlook are you using to make such a determination?
3. When cultural relativists say that every culture should embrace a policy of tolerance, are they contradicting themselves? If so, how? If cultural relativism were true, would this fact make wars between societies less or more likely? Explain.
4. According to a cultural relativist, would the civil rights reforms that Martin Luther King Jr. sought be morally right or wrong? Do *you* think that his efforts at reform were morally wrong? Why or why not?
5. If you traveled the world and saw that cultures differ dramatically in their moral judgments, would you conclude from this evidence that cultural relativism was true? Why or why not?
6. Suppose a serial killer approves of his murderous actions. According to subjective relativism, are the killer's actions therefore justified? Do *you* believe the serial killer's murders are justified? If not, is your judgment based on a subjective relativist's perspective or an objectivist perspective? Explain.
7. Are you a cultural relativist? Why or why not?

8. Suppose a deer that had been shot by a hunter writhed in agony for days before dying. You exclaim, "How she must have suffered! Her horrendous pain was a bad thing." In this situation, does the word *bad* refer to any moral properties? Is there really something bad about the deer's suffering—or is your use of the word just a way to express your horror without making any moral statement at all? Explain your answers.

ETHICAL DILEMMAS

1. In Western societies, some cultural subgroups believe it is morally permissible to kill anyone who criticizes their religion. Do you agree or disagree with this view? On what grounds? Is your position relativist or objectivist?
2. Suppose you are a social reformer campaigning against your culture's practice of systematically discriminating against the poorest people in your society. Do you think your stance is morally right—or is your culture right while you are wrong? Why?
3. Suppose you accept (approve of) premarital sex. Is it possible for you to be mistaken about this issue? Why or why not? Does your answer suggest that you are a subjective relativist?

Endnotes

1. Walter T. Stace, *The Concept of Morals* (1937; reprint, New York: Macmillan, 1965), 8–58.
2. Phillip Montague, "Are There Objective and Absolute Moral Standards?" in *Reason and Responsibility: Readings in Some Basic Problems in Philosophy,* 5th ed., ed. Joel Feinberg (Belmont, CA: Wadsworth, 1978), 490–91.
3. Solomon Asch, *Social Psychology* (Englewood Cliffs, NJ: Prentice-Hall, 1952), 378–79.
4. See, for example, Clyde Kluckhohn, "Ethical Relativity: Sic et Non," *Journal of Philosophy* 52 (1955): 663–77, and E. O. Wilson, *On Human Nature* (1978; reprint, New York: Bantam, 1979).
5. A. J. Ayer, "Critique of Ethics and Theology," in *Language, Truth and Logic* (1936; reprint, New York: Dover, 1952), 107.
6. Ayer, "Critique of Ethics," 112.
7. This scenario is inspired by some of Brand Blanshard's examples from "Emotivism," in *Reason and Goodness* (1961; reprint, New York: G. Allen & Unwin, 1978).
8. Blanshard, "Emotivism," 204–5.

CHAPTER 3

Moral Arguments

This much is clear: we cannot escape the ethical facts of life. We often must make moral judgments, assess moral principles or rules, contend with moral theories, and argue the pros and cons of moral issues. Typically we do all of these things believing that in one way or another they *really matter*.

Because we think that ethics (that is, moral *philosophy*) matters, it follows that moral *reasoning* matters, for we could make little headway in these difficult waters without the use of reasons and arguments. Along the way we may take into account our feelings, desires, beliefs, and other factors, but getting to our destination depends mostly on the quality of our moral reasoning. Through moral reasoning we assess what is right and wrong, good and bad, virtuous and vicious. We make and dismantle arguments for this view and for that. In our finest moments, we follow the lead of reason in the search for answers, trying to rise above subjectivism, prejudice, and confusion.

In this chapter you will discover (if you haven't already) that you are no stranger to moral reasoning. Moral reasoning is ordinary critical reasoning applied to ethics. Critical reasoning (or critical thinking) is the careful, systematic evaluation of statements or claims. We use critical reasoning every day to determine whether a statement is worthy of acceptance—that is, whether it is true. We harness critical reasoning to assess the truth of all sorts of claims in all kinds of contexts—personal, professional, academic, philosophical, scientific, political, and ethical. Moral reasoning, then, is a type of reasoning that you have experienced before.

We therefore begin this chapter with the basics of critical reasoning. The focus is on the skills that are at the heart of this kind of thinking—the formulation and evaluation of logical arguments. The rest of the chapter is about applying critical reasoning to the claims and arguments of ethics.

CLAIMS AND ARGUMENTS

When you use critical reasoning, your ultimate aim is usually to figure out whether to accept, or believe, a statement—either someone else's statement or one of your own. A **statement**, or claim, is an assertion that something is or is not the case, that it is either true or false. These are statements:

- The ship sailed on the wind-tossed sea.
- I feel tired and listless.
- Murder is wrong.
- 5 + 5 = 10.
- A circle is not a square.

These statements assert that something is or is not the case. Whether you accept them, reject them, or neither, they are still statements because they are assertions that can be either true or false.

The following, however, are not statements. They do not assert that something is or is not the case:

- Why is Anna laughing?
- Is abortion immoral?
- Hand me the screwdriver.
- Don't speak to me.
- Hello, Webster.
- For heaven's sake!

A fundamental principle of critical reasoning is that we should not accept a statement as true without good reasons. If a statement is supported by good reasons, we are entitled to believe it. The better the reasons supporting a statement, the more likely it is to be true. Our acceptance of a statement, then, can vary in strength. If a statement is supported by strong reasons, we are entitled to believe it strongly. If it is supported by weaker reasons, our belief should likewise be weaker. If the reasons are equivocal—if they do not help us decide one way or another—we should suspend judgment until the evidence is more definitive.

Reasons supporting a statement are themselves statements. To lend credence to another claim, these supporting statements may assert something about scientific evidence, expert opinion, relevant examples, or other considerations. In this way they provide reasons for believing that a statement is true, that what is asserted is actual. When this state of affairs exists—when at least one statement attempts to provide reasons for believing another statement—we have an **argument**. An argument is a group of statements, one of which is supposed to be supported by the rest. An argument in this sense, of course, has nothing to do with the common notion of arguments as quarrels or shouting matches.

In an argument, the supporting statements are known as **premises**; the statement being supported is known as a **conclusion**. Consider these arguments:

> *Argument 1.* Capital punishment is morally permissible because it helps to deter crime.

> *Argument 2.* If John killed Bill in self-defense, he did not commit murder. He did act in self-defense. Therefore, he did not commit murder.

> *Argument 3.* Telling a white lie is morally permissible. We should judge the rightness of an act by its impact on human well-being. If an act increases human well-being, then it is right. Without question, telling a white lie increases human well-being because it spares people's feelings; that's what white lies are for.

These arguments are fairly simple. In Argument 1, a single premise ("because it helps to deter crime") supports a straightforward conclusion ("Capital punishment is morally permissible"). Argument 2 has two premises: "If John killed Bill in self-defense, he did not commit murder" and "He did act in self-defense." And the conclusion is "Therefore, he did not commit murder." Argument 3 has three premises: "We should judge the rightness of an act by its impact on human well-being," "If an act increases human well-being, then it is right," and "Without question, telling a white lie increases human well-being because it spares people's feelings." Its conclusion is "Telling a white lie is morally permissible."

As you can see, these three arguments have different structures. Argument 1, for example, has just one premise, but Arguments 2 and 3 have two and three premises. In Arguments 1 and 3, the conclusion is stated first; in Argument 2, last. Obviously, arguments can vary dramatically in their number of premises, in the placement of premises and conclusion, and in the wording of each of these parts. But all arguments share a common pattern: at least one premise is intended to support a conclusion. This pattern is what makes an argument an argument.

Despite the simplicity of this premise-conclusion arrangement, though, arguments are not always easy to identify. They can be embedded in long passages of nonargumentative prose, and nonargumentative prose can often look like arguments. Consider:

> The number of abortions performed in this state is increasing. More and more women say that they favor greater access to abortion. This is an outrage.

Do you see an argument in this passage? You shouldn't, because there is none. The first two sentences are meant to be assertions of fact, and the last one is an expression of indignation. There is no premise providing reasons to accept a conclusion. But what if we altered the passage to make it an argument? Look:

> The number of abortions performed in this state is increasing, and more and more women say that they favor greater access to abortion. Therefore, in this state the trend among women is toward greater acceptance of abortion.

This is now an argument. There is a conclusion ("Therefore, in this state the trend among women is toward greater acceptance of abortion") supported by two premises ("The number of abortions performed in this state is increasing," and "more and more women say that they favor greater access to abortion"). We are given reasons for accepting a claim.

Notice how easy it would be to elaborate on the nonargumentative version, adding other unsupported claims and more expressions of the writer's attitude toward the subject matter. We would end up with a much longer passage piled high with more assertions—but with no argument in sight. Often those who write such passages believe that because they have stated their opinion, they have presented an argument. But a bundle of unsupported claims—however clearly stated—does not an argument make. Only when at least one reason is given for believing one of these claims is an argument made.

Learning to distinguish arguments from nonargumentative material takes practice. The job gets easier, however, if you pay attention to **indicator words**. Indicator words are terms that often appear in arguments and signal that a premise or conclusion may be nearby. Notice that in the argument about abortion, the word *therefore* indicates that the conclusion follows, and in Argument 1 the word *because* signals the beginning of a premise. In addition to *therefore*, common conclusion indicators include *consequently, hence, it follows that, thus, so, it must be that*, and *as a result*. Besides *because*, some common premise indicators are *since, for, given that, due to the fact that, for the reason that, the reason being, assuming that*, and *as indicated by*.

Understand that indicator words are not foolproof evidence that a premise or conclusion is near. Sometimes words that often function as indicators appear when no argument at all is present. Indicator words are simply hints that an argument may be close by.

Probably the most reliable way to identify arguments is to *always look for the conclusion first*. When you know what claim is being supported, you can more easily see what statements are doing the supporting. A true argument always has something to prove. If there is no statement that the writer is trying to convince you to accept, no argument is present.

Finally, understand that *argumentation* (the presentation of an argument) is not the same thing as *persuasion*. To offer a good argument is to present reasons why a particular assertion is true. To persuade someone of something is to influence her opinion by any number of means, including emotional appeals, linguistic or rhetorical tricks, deception, threats, propaganda, and more. Reasoned argument does not necessarily play any part at all in persuasion. You may be able to use some of these ploys to persuade people to believe a claim. But if you do, you will not have established that the claim is worth believing. On the other hand, if you articulate a good argument, then you prove something—and others just might be persuaded by your reasoning.

ARGUMENTS GOOD AND BAD

A good argument shows that its conclusion is worthy of belief or acceptance; a bad argument fails to show this. A good argument gives you good reasons to accept a claim; a bad argument proves nothing. So the crucial question is, How can you tell which is which? To start, you can learn more about different kinds of arguments and how they get to be good or bad.

There are two basic types of arguments: **deductive** and **inductive**. Deductive arguments are supposed to give logically conclusive support to their conclusions. Inductive arguments, on the other hand, are supposed to offer only probable support for their conclusions.

Consider this classic deductive argument:

All men are mortal.

Socrates is a man.

Therefore, Socrates is mortal.

It is deductive because the support offered for the conclusion is meant to be absolutely unshakable. When a deductive argument actually achieves this kind of conclusive support, it is said to be **valid**. In a valid argument, if the premises are true, then the conclusion absolutely has to be true. In the Socrates argument, if the premises are true, the conclusion *must be true*. The conclusion follows inexorably from the premises. The argument is therefore valid. When a deductive argument does not offer conclusive support for the conclusion, it is said to be **invalid**. In an invalid argument, it is not the case that if the premises are true, the conclusion must be true. Suppose the Socrates argument was changed to the following:

All men are mortal.

Socrates is mortal.

Therefore, Socrates is a man.

Then the argument would be invalid because even if the premises were true, the conclusion would not necessarily be true. (If, for example, "Socrates" in this case was the name of my pet dog, the second premise would still be true but the conclusion clearly would not be.) The conclusion would not follow inexorably from the premises.

Notice that the validity or invalidity of an argument is a matter of its *form*, not its content. The structure of a deductive argument renders it either valid or invalid, and validity is a separate matter from the truth of the argument's statements. Its statements (premises and conclusion) may be either true or false, but that has nothing to do with validity. Saying that an argument is valid means that it has a particular form that ensures that if the premises are true, the conclusion can be nothing but true. There is no way that the premises can be true and the conclusion false.

Recall that there are indicator words that point to the presence of premises and conclusions. There are also indicator words that suggest (but do not prove) that an argument is deductive. Some of the more common terms are *it necessarily follows that, it must be the case that, it logically follows that, conclusively,* and *necessarily.*

Now let us turn to inductive arguments. Examine this one:

Almost all the men at this college have high SAT scores.

Therefore, Julio (a male student at the college) probably has high SAT scores.

This argument is inductive because it is intended to provide *probable,* not decisive, support to the conclusion. That is, the argument is intended to show only that, at best, the conclusion is probably true. With any inductive argument, it is possible for the premises to be true and the conclusion false. An inductive argument that manages to give probable support to the conclusion is said to be **strong**. In a strong argument, if the premises are true, the conclusion is probably true (more likely to be true than not). The SAT argument is strong. An inductive argument that does not give probable support to the conclusion is said to be **weak**. In a weak argument, if the premises are true, the conclusion is not probable (not more likely to be true than not true). If we change the first premise in the SAT argument to "Twenty percent of the men at this college have high SAT scores," the argument would be weak.

Like deductive arguments, inductive ones are often accompanied by indicator words. These terms include *probably, likely, in all probability, it is reasonable to suppose that, odds are,* and *chances are.*

Good arguments provide you with good reasons for believing their conclusions. You now know that good arguments must be valid or strong. But they must also have true premises. Good arguments must have both the right form (be valid or strong) and reliable content (have true premises). Any argument that fails in either of these respects is a bad argument. A valid argument with true premises is said to be **sound**; a strong argument with true premises is said to be **cogent**.

To evaluate an argument is to determine whether it is good or not, and establishing this requires you to check the argument's form and the truth of its premises. You can check the truth of premises in many different ways. Sometimes you can see immediately that a premise is true (or false). At other times you may need to examine a premise more closely or even do some research. Assessing an argument's form is also usually a very straightforward process. With inductive arguments, sometimes common sense is all that is required to determine whether they are strong or weak (whether the conclusions follow from the premises). With deductive arguments, just thinking about how the premises are related to the conclusion is often sufficient. In all cases the key to correctly and efficiently determining the validity or strength of arguments is practice.

Fortunately, there are some techniques that can improve your ability to check the validity of deductive arguments. Some deductive forms are so common that just being familiar with them can give you a big advantage. Let's look at some of them.

To begin, understand that you can easily indicate an argument's form by using a kind of standard shorthand, with letters standing for statements. Consider, for example, this argument:

If Maria walks to work, then she will be late.

She is walking to work.

Therefore, she will be late.

Here's how we symbolize this argument's form:

If p, then q.

p.

Therefore, q.

We represent each statement with a letter, thereby laying bare the argument's skeletal form. The first premise is a compound statement, consisting of two constituent statements, p and q. This particular argument form is known as a *conditional*. A conditional argument has at least one conditional premise—a premise in an if-then pattern (If p, then q). The two parts of a conditional premise are known as the *antecedent* (which begins with *if*) and the *consequent* (which follows *then*).

This argument form happens to be very common—so common that it has a name, **modus ponens**, or "affirming the antecedent." The first premise is conditional ("If Maria walks to work, then she will be late"), and the second premise affirms the antecedent of that conditional ("She is walking to work"). This form is *always valid*: if the premises are true, the conclusion *has to be true*. Any argument that has this form will be valid regardless of the subject matter.

Another frequently occurring form is known as **modus tollens**, or "denying the consequent":

If Maria walks to work, then she will be late.

She will not be late.

Therefore, she will not walk to work.

Symbolized, *modus tollens* looks like this:

If p, then q.

Not q.

Therefore, not p.

Modus tollens is always valid, no matter what statements you plug into the formula.

Here are two more common argument forms. These, however, are *always invalid*.

Denying the antecedent:

If Maria walks to work, then she will be late.

She will not walk to work.

Therefore, she will not be late.

If p, then q.

Not p.

Therefore, not q.

Affirming the consequent:

If Maria walks to work, then she will be late.

She will be late.

Therefore, she will walk to work.

If *p*, then *q*.

q.

Therefore, *p*.

Do you see the problem with these two? In the first one (denying the antecedent), even a false antecedent (if Maria will not walk to work) doesn't mean that she will not be late. Maybe she will sit at home and be late, or be late for some other reason. When the antecedent is denied, the premises can be true and the conclusion false—clearly an invalid argument. In the second argument (affirming the consequent), even a true consequent (if Maria will be late) doesn't mean that she will walk to work. Some other factor besides her walking could cause Maria to be late. Again, the premises can be true while the conclusion is false—definitely invalid.

Consider one last form, the **hypothetical syllogism** (*hypothetical* means *conditional*; a *syllogism* is a three-statement deductive argument):

If Maria walks to work, then she will be late.

If she is late, she will be fired.

Therefore, if Maria walks to work, she will be fired.

If *p*, then *q*.

If *q*, then *r*.

Therefore, if *p*, then *r*.

The hypothetical syllogism is a valid argument form. If the premises are true, the conclusion must be true.

Obviously, if *modus ponens*, *modus tollens*, and the hypothetical syllogism are always valid, then any arguments you encounter that have the same form will also be valid. And if denying the antecedent and affirming the consequent are always invalid, any arguments you come across that have the same form will also be invalid. The best way to make use of these facts is to memorize each argument form so you can tell right away when an argument matches one of them—and thereby see immediately whether it is valid or invalid.

But what if you bump into a deductive argument that does not match one of these common forms? You can try the *counterexample method*. This approach is based on a fundamental fact that you already know: *it is impossible for a valid argument to have true premises and a false conclusion*. So to test the validity of an argument, you first invent a twin argument that has exactly the same form as the argument you are examining, but you try to give this new argument true premises and a false conclusion. If you can construct such an argument, you have proven that your original argument is invalid.

Suppose you want to test this argument for validity:

> If capital punishment deters crime, then the number of death row inmates will decrease over time.
>
> But capital punishment does not deter crime.
>
> Therefore, the number of death row inmates will not decrease over time.

You can probably see right away that this argument is an example of denying the antecedent, an invalid form. But for the sake of example, let's use the counterexample method in this case. Suppose we come up with this twin argument:

> If lizards are mammals, then they have legs.
>
> But they are not mammals.
>
> Therefore, they do not have legs.

We have invented a twin argument that has true premises and a false conclusion, so we know that the original argument is invalid.

IMPLIED PREMISES

Most of the arguments that we encounter in everyday life are embedded in larger tracts of nonargumentative prose—in essays, reports, letters to the editor, editorials, and the like. The challenge is to pick out the premises and conclusions and evaluate the assembled arguments. In many cases, though, there is an additional obstacle: some premises may be implied instead of stated. Sometimes the premises are implicit because they are too obvious to mention; readers mentally fill in the blanks. But in most cases, implicit premises should not be left unstated. It is often unclear what premises have been assumed; and unless these are spelled out, argument evaluation becomes difficult or impossible. More to the point, unstated premises are often the most dubious parts of an argument. This problem is especially common in moral arguments, where the implicit premises are frequently the most controversial and the most in need of close scrutiny.

Here is a typical argument with an unstated premise:

The use of condoms is completely unnatural. They have been manufactured for the explicit purpose of interfering in the natural process of procreation. Therefore, the use of condoms should be banned.

In this argument, the first two sentences constitute a single premise, the gist of which is that using condoms is unnatural. The conclusion is that the use of condoms should be banned. This conclusion, however, does not follow from the stated premise. There is a logical gap between premise and conclusion. The argument will work only if the missing premise is supplied. Here's a good possibility: "Anything that interferes in a natural process should not be allowed." The argument then becomes:

The use of condoms is completely unnatural. They have been manufactured for the explicit purpose of interfering in the natural process of procreation. Anything that interferes in a natural process should not be allowed. Therefore, the use of condoms should be banned.

By adding the implicit premise, we have filled out the argument, making it valid and a little less mysterious. But now that the missing premise has been made explicit, we can see that it is dubious or, at least, controversial. Should everything that interferes in a natural process be banned? If so, we would have to ban antibiotics, cancer drugs, deodorants, and automobiles. (Later in this chapter, ways to judge the truth of moral premises are discussed.)

When you evaluate an argument, you should try to explicitly state any implied premise (or premises) when (1) there seems to be a logical gap between premises or between premises and the conclusion, and (2) the missing material is not a commonsense assumption. In general, the supplied premise should make the argument valid (when the argument is supposed to be deductive) or strong (when the argument is supposed to be inductive). It should also be *plausible* (as close to the truth as possible) and *fitting* (coinciding with what you think is the author's intent). The point of these stipulations is that when you supply a missing premise, you should be fair and honest, expressing it in such a way that the argument is as solid as possible and in keeping with the author's purpose. Adding a premise that renders an argument ridiculous is easy, and so is distorting the author's intent—and with neither tack are you likely to learn anything or uncover the truth.

Be aware, though, that some arguments are irredeemably bad, and no supplied premise that is properly made can save them. They cannot be turned into good arguments without altering them beyond recognition or original intent. You need not take these arguments seriously, and the responsibility of recasting them lies with those who offer them.

MORAL STATEMENTS AND ARGUMENTS

When we deliberate about the rightness of our actions, make careful moral judgments about the character or behavior of others, or strive to resolve complex ethical issues, we are usually making or critiquing moral arguments—or trying to. And rightly so. To a remarkable degree, moral arguments are the vehicles that move ethical thinking and discourse along. The rest of this chapter should give you a demonstration of how far your skills in devising and evaluating moral arguments can take you.

Recall that arguments are made up of statements (premises and conclusions), and thus moral arguments are, too. What makes an argument a moral argument is that its conclusion is always a moral statement. A **moral statement** is a statement affirming that an action is right or wrong or that a person (or one's motive or character) is good or bad. These are moral statements:

- Capital punishment is wrong.
- Jena should not have lied.
- You ought to treat him as he treated you.
- Tania is a good person.
- Cruelty to animals is immoral.

Notice the use of the terms *wrong, should, ought, good,* and *immoral.* Such words are the mainstays of moral discourse, though some of them (for example, *good* and *wrong*) are also used in nonmoral senses.

Nonmoral statements are very different. They do not affirm that an action is right or wrong or that a person is good or bad. They assert that a state of affairs is actual (true or false) but do not assign a moral value to it. Most of the statements that we encounter every day are nonmoral. Of course, nonmoral statements may assert nonmoral normative judgments, such as "This is a good library" or "Jack ought to invest in stocks," but these are clearly not moral statements. They may also describe a state of affairs that touches on moral concerns, without *being* moral statements themselves. For example:

- Many people think that capital punishment is wrong.
- Jena did not lie.
- You treated him as he treated you.
- Tania tries to be a good person.
- Animals are treated cruelly.

Now we can be more specific about the structure of moral arguments. A typical moral argument consists of premises and a conclusion, just as any other kind of argument does, with the conclusion being a moral statement, or judgment. The premises, however, are a combination of the moral and nonmoral. At least one premise must be a moral statement affirming a moral principle or rule (a general moral standard), and at least one premise must be a nonmoral statement about a state of affairs, usually a specific type of action. Beyond these simple requirements, the structure of moral arguments can vary in standard ways: there may be many premises or few; premises may be implicit or explicit; and extraneous material may be present or absent. Take a look at this moral argument:

1. Committing a violent act to defend yourself against physical attack is morally permissible.
2. Assaulting someone who is attacking you is a violent act of self-defense.
3. Therefore, assaulting someone who is attacking you is morally permissible.

Premise 1 is a moral statement asserting a general moral principle about the rightness of a category of actions (violent acts in self-defense). Premise 2 is a nonmoral statement about the characteristics of a specific kind of action (violent acts against someone who is attacking you). It asserts that a specific kind of action falls under the general moral principle expressed in Premise 1. Premise 3, the conclusion, is a moral judgment about the rightness of the specific kind of action in light of the general moral principle.

Why must we have at least one premise that is a moral statement? Without a moral premise, the argument would not get off the ground. We cannot infer a moral statement (conclusion) from a nonmoral statement (premise). That is, we cannot reason that a moral statement must be true because a nonmoral state of affairs is actual. Or as philosophers say, we cannot establish what *ought to be* or *should be* based solely on what *is*. What if our self-defense argument contained no moral premise? Look:

2. Assaulting a person who is attacking you is a violent act of self-defense.

3. Therefore, assaulting a person who is attacking you is morally permissible.

The conclusion no longer follows. It says something about the rightness of an action, but the premise asserts nothing about rightness—it just characterizes the nonmoral aspects of an action. Perhaps the action described is morally permissible or perhaps it is not—Premise 2 does not say.

Another example:

1. Not using every medical means available to keep a seriously ill newborn infant alive is allowing the infant to die.

3. Therefore, not using every medical means available to keep a seriously ill newborn infant alive is wrong.

As it stands, this argument is seriously flawed. The conclusion (a moral statement) does not follow from the nonmoral premise. Even if we know that "not using every medical means" is equivalent to allowing a seriously ill newborn to die, we cannot then conclude that the action is wrong. We need a premise making that assertion:

2. Allowing terminally ill newborn infants to die is wrong.

Here's the complete argument:

1. Not using every medical means available to keep a seriously ill newborn infant alive is allowing the infant to die.

2. Allowing terminally ill newborn infants to die is wrong.

3. Therefore, not using every medical means available to keep a seriously ill newborn infant alive is wrong.

A nonmoral premise is also necessary in a moral argument. Why exactly? Recall that the conclusion of a typical moral argument is a moral judgment, or claim, about a particular kind of action. The moral premise is a general moral principle, or standard, concerning a wider category of actions. But we cannot infer a statement (conclusion) about a *particular kind of action* from a moral statement (premise) about a *broad category of actions* unless we have a nonmoral premise to link the two. We saw, for example, that we cannot infer from the general principle that "committing a violent act to defend yourself . . . is morally permissible" the conclusion that "assaulting a person who is attacking you is morally permissible" unless a nonmoral premise tells us that assaulting a person who is attacking you is an instance of self-defense. (The nonmoral premise may seem obvious here, but not everyone would agree that violence against a person who is attacking you is an example of self-defense. Some might claim that such violence is an unnecessary act of retaliation or revenge.) The role of the nonmoral premise, then, is to affirm that the general moral principle does indeed apply to the particular case.

Unfortunately, both moral and nonmoral premises are often left unstated in moral arguments. As we noted earlier, making implicit premises explicit is always a good idea, but in moral arguments it is critical. The unseen premises (an argument may have several) are the ones most likely to be dubious or unfounded, a problem that can arise whether an argument is yours or someone else's. Too often, unstated premises are assumptions that you may be barely aware of; they might be the true, unacknowledged source of disagreement between you and others. No premise should be left unexamined.

The general guidelines discussed earlier about uncovering unstated premises apply to moral arguments—but we need to add a proviso. Remember, in a moral argument, as in any other kind of argument, you have good reason to look for implicit premises if there is a logical gap between premises, and the missing premise is not simply common sense. And any premise you supply should be both plausible and fitting. But note: The easiest way to identify implied premises in a moral argument is to treat it as *deductive*. Approaching moral arguments this way helps you not only find implied premises but also assess the worth of *all* the premises.

For example:

1. The use of capital punishment does not deter crime.

2. Therefore, the use of capital punishment is immoral.

This is an invalid argument. Even if the premise is true, the conclusion does not follow from it. The argument needs a premise that can bridge the gap between the current premise and the conclusion. So we should ask, "What premise can we add that will be plausible and fitting *and* make the argument valid?" This premise will do: "Administering a punishment to criminals that does not deter crime is immoral." The argument then becomes:

1. Administering a punishment to criminals that does not deter crime is immoral.
2. The use of capital punishment does not deter crime.
3. Therefore, the use of capital punishment is immoral.

Now the argument is valid, and trying to make it valid has helped us find at least one premise that might work. Moreover, if we know that the argument is valid, we can focus our inquiry on the truth of the premises. After all, if there is something wrong with a valid argument (that is, if the argument is not sound), we know that the trouble is in the premises—specifically, that at least one premise must be false. To put it another way, whether or not such an argument is a good argument depends entirely on the truth of the premises.

As it turns out, our added premise is a general moral principle. And like many implied premises, it is questionable. Deterrence is not necessarily the only reason for administering punishment. Some would say that justice is a better reason; others, that rehabilitation is. (The second premise is also dubious, but we won't worry about that now.)

In any case, if the supplied premise renders the argument valid, and if the premise is plausible and fitting, we can then conclude that we have filled out the argument properly. We can then examine the resulting argument and either accept or reject it. And if we wish to explore the issue in greater depth, we can overhaul the argument altogether to see what we can learn. We can radically change or add premises until we have a sound argument or at least a valid one with plausible premises.

TESTING MORAL PREMISES

But how can we evaluate moral premises? After all, we cannot check them by consulting a scientific study or opinion poll as we might when examining nonmoral premises. Usually the best approach is to use counterexamples.

If we want to test a universal generalization such as "All dogs have tails," we can look for counterexamples—instances that prove the generalization false. All we have to do to show that the statement "All dogs have tails" is false is to find one tailless dog. And a thorough search for tailless dogs is a way to check the generalization. Likewise, if we want to test a moral premise (a variety of universal generalization), we can look for counterexamples.

Examine this valid moral argument:

1. Causing a person's death is wrong.
2. Individuals in a deep, irreversible coma are incapacitated persons.
3. "Pulling the plug" on someone in a deep, irreversible coma is causing a person to die.
4. Therefore, "pulling the plug" on someone in a deep, irreversible coma is wrong.

Premise 1 is the moral premise, a general moral principle about killing. Premises 2 and 3 are nonmoral premises. (Premise 2 is entailed by Premise 3, but we separate the two to emphasize the importance to this argument of the concept of personhood.) Statement 4, of course, is the conclusion, the verdict that causing someone in a deep coma to die is immoral.

Is Premise 1 true? It is at least dubious, because counterexamples abound in which the principle seems false. Is it wrong to kill one person to save a hundred? Is it wrong to kill a person in self-defense? Is it wrong to kill a person in wartime? As it stands, Premise 1 seems implausible.

To salvage the argument, we can revise Premise 1 (as well as Premise 3) to try to make it impervious to counterexamples. We can change it like this:

1. Causing the death of a person who is incapacitated is wrong.
2. Individuals in a deep, irreversible coma are persons.
3. "Pulling the plug" on someone in a deep, irreversible coma is causing an incapacitated person to die.
4. Therefore, "pulling the plug" on someone in a deep, irreversible coma is wrong.

Premise 1 now seems a bit more reasonable. In its current form, it rules out the counterexamples involving self-defense and war. But it does not escape the killing-to-save-lives counterexample. In some circumstances it may be morally permissible to kill someone to save many others, even if the person is incapacitated. To get around this problem, we can amend Premise 1 so the counterexample is no longer a threat (and make a corresponding change in the conclusion). For example:

1. Causing the death of a person who is incapacitated is wrong, except to save lives.
2. Individuals in a deep, irreversible coma are persons.
3. "Pulling the plug" on someone in a deep, irreversible coma is causing an incapacitated person to die.
4. Therefore, "pulling the plug" on someone in a deep, irreversible coma is wrong, except to save lives.

Premise 1 now seems much closer to being correct than before. It may not be flawless, but it is much improved. By considering counterexamples, we have made the whole argument better.

Checking a moral premise against possible counterexamples is a way to consult our **considered moral judgments**, a topic we look at more closely in the next chapter. Our considered moral judgments are those that are as free from bias and distorting passions as possible, judgments that we generally trust unless there is a reason to doubt them. If such judgments are at odds with a moral premise that is based on a cherished moral principle or moral theory, we may have, on the face of it, a reason to doubt not only the premise but also the principle or theory from which it is derived. We may then need to reexamine the claims involved and how they are related. If we do, we may find that our judgments are on solid ground and the premise, principle, or theory needs to be adjusted—or vice versa. If our purpose is solely to evaluate a moral premise in an argument, we need not carry our investigation this far. But we should understand that widening our investigation may sometimes be appropriate and that our moral beliefs are often more interconnected than we might realize. Our ultimate goal should be to ensure that all our moral beliefs are as logically consistent as we can make them.

ASSESSING NONMORAL PREMISES

Sometimes the sticking point in a moral argument is not a moral premise but a nonmoral one—a claim about a nonmoral state of affairs. Often, people on both sides of a dispute may agree on a moral principle but differ dramatically on the nonmoral facts. Usually these facts concern the consequences of an action or the characteristics of the parties involved. Does pornography cause people to commit sex crimes? Does capital punishment deter crime? Is a depressed person competent to decide whether to commit suicide? When does the fetus become viable outside of the womb? Are African Americans underrepresented among executives in corporate America? Does gay marriage undermine the institution of heterosexual marriage? These and countless other questions arise—and must be answered—as we try to develop and analyze moral arguments.

The most important principle to remember is that nonmoral premises, like all premises, *must be supported by good reasons*. As we have already seen, simply believing or asserting a claim does not make it so. We should insist that our own nonmoral premises and those of others be backed by reliable scientific research, the opinions of trustworthy experts, pertinent examples and analogies, historical records, or our own background knowledge (claims that we have excellent reasons to believe).

Ensuring that nonmoral premises are supported by good reasons is sometimes difficult but always worth the effort. The process begins by simply asking, "Is this statement true?" and "What reasons do I have for believing this?"

In your search for answers, keep the following in mind:

1. *Use reliable sources.* If you have reason to doubt the accuracy of a source, do not use it. Doubt it if it produces statements you know to be false, ignores reliable data (such as the latest scientific research), or has a track record of presenting inaccurate information or dubious arguments. Make sure that any experts you rely on are in fact experts in their chosen field. In general, true experts have the requisite education and training, the relevant experience in making reliable judgments, and a good reputation among peers.

   Probably every major moral issue discussed in this book is associated with numerous advocacy groups, each one devoted to promoting its particular view of things. Too often the information coming from many of these groups is unreliable. Do not automatically assume otherwise. Double-check any information you get from them with sources you know are reliable and see if this information is supported by scientific studies, expert opinion, or other evidence.

2. *Beware when evidence conflicts.* You have good reason to doubt a statement if it conflicts with other statements you think are well supported. If your nonmoral premise is inconsistent with another claim you believe is true, you cannot simply choose the one you like best. To resolve the conflict, you must evaluate them both by weighing the evidence for each one.

3. *Let reason rule.* Deliberating on moral issues is serious business, often involving the questioning of cherished views and the stirring of strong feelings. Many times the temptation to dispense with reason and blindly embrace a favorite outlook is enormous. This common—and very human—predicament can lead us to veer far from the relevant evidence and true nonmoral premises. Specifically, we may reject or disregard evidence that conflicts with what we most want to believe. We may even try to pretend that the conflicting evidence actually supports our preconceptions. Yet resisting the relevant evidence is just one side of the coin. We may also look for and therefore find only the evidence that supports what we want to believe, going around the world to confirm our prejudices.

Our best chance to avert these tendencies is to try hard to be both critical and fair—to make a deliberate effort to examine *all* the relevant evidence, the information both for and against our preferred beliefs. After all, the point of assessing a moral argument is to discover the truth. We must be brave enough to let the evidence point where it will.

AVOIDING BAD ARGUMENTS

Recall that a good argument has true premises plus a conclusion that follows from those premises. A bad argument fails at least one of these conditions—it has a false premise or a conclusion that does not follow. This failure, however, can appear in many different argument forms, some of which are extremely common. These commonly bad arguments are known as **fallacies**. They are so distinctive and are used so often that they have been given names and are usually covered in courses on critical reasoning. Though flawed, fallacies are often persuasive and frequently employed to mislead the unwary—even in (or *especially* in) moral reasoning. The best way to avoid using fallacies—or being taken in by them—is to study them so you know how they work and can easily identify them. The following is a brief review of some fallacies that are most prevalent in moral argumentation.

Begging the Question

Begging the question is the fallacy of arguing in a circle—that is, trying to use a statement as both a premise in an argument and the conclusion of that argument. Such an argument says, in effect, *p* is true because *p* is true. This kind of reasoning, of course, proves nothing.

For example:

1. Women in Muslim countries, regardless of their social status and economic limitations, are entitled to certain rights, including but not necessarily limited to suffrage.

2. Therefore, all women in Muslim countries have the right to vote in political elections.

This argument is equivalent to saying "Women in Muslim countries have a right to vote because women in Muslim countries have a right to vote." The conclusion merely repeats the premise but in different words. The best protection against circular reasoning is a close reading of the argument.

Equivocation

The fallacy of **equivocation** assigns two different meanings to the same term in an argument. Here's an example that, in one form or another, is a commonplace in the abortion debate:

1. A fetus is indisputably human.

2. A human is endowed with rights that cannot be invalidated, including a right to life.

3. Therefore, a fetus has a right to life.

This argument equivocates on the word *human*. In Premise 1, the term means physiologically human, as in having human DNA. This claim, of course, is indeed indisputable. But in Premise 2, *human* is used in the sense of *person*—that is, an individual having full moral rights. Because the premises refer to two different things, the conclusion does not follow. If you are not paying close attention, though, you might not detect the equivocation and accept the argument as it is.

Appeal to Authority

This fallacy is relying on the opinion of someone thought to be an expert who is not. An expert, of course, can be a source of reliable information, but only if he or she really is an authority in the designated subject area. A true expert is someone who is both knowledgeable about the facts and able to make reliable judgments about them. Ultimately, experts are experts because they carefully base their opinions on the available evidence.

We make a fallacious **appeal to authority** when we (1) cite experts who are not experts in the field under discussion (though they may be experts in some other field) or (2) cite nonexperts as experts. Expertise in one field does not automatically carry over to another, and even nonexperts who are prestigious and famous are still just nonexperts. In general, on subjects outside an expert's area of expertise, his or her opinions are no more reliable than those of nonexperts.

Two rules of thumb should guide your use of expert opinion. First, if a claim conflicts with the consensus of opinion among experts, you have good reason to doubt the claim. Second, if experts disagree about a claim, you again have good reason to doubt it.

Slippery Slope

Slippery slope is the fallacy of using dubious premises to argue that doing a particular action will inevitably lead to other actions that will result in disaster, so you should not do the first action. This way of arguing is perfectly legitimate if the premises are solid—that is, if there are good reasons to believe that the first step really will lead to ruin. Consider:

1. Rampant proliferation of pornography on the Internet leads to obsession with pornographic materials.
2. Obsession with pornographic materials disrupts relationships, and this disruption leads to divorce.
3. Therefore, we should ban pornography on the Internet.

Perhaps the chain of events laid out here could actually occur, but we have been given no reason to believe that it would. (You can see that this argument is also missing a moral premise.) Scientific evidence showing that this sequence of cause and effect does occur as described would constitute good reason to accept Premises 1 and 2.

Appeal to Emotion

Emotions have a role to play in the moral life. In moral arguments, however, the use of emotions alone as substitutes for premises is a fallacy. We commit this **appeal to emotion** fallacy when we try to convince someone to accept a conclusion not by providing them with relevant reasons but by appealing only to fear, guilt, anger, hate, compassion, and the like. For example:

> The defendant is obviously guilty of murder in this case. Look at him in the courtroom—he's terrifying and menacing. And no one can ignore the way he stabbed that girl and mutilated her body. And her poor parents . . .

The question here is whether the defendant committed the crime, and the feelings of fear and pity that he evokes are not relevant to it. But if the question were about the anguish or torment inflicted on the victim or her parents, then our feelings of empathy would indeed be relevant—and so would any pertinent moral principles or theories.

Faulty Analogy

The use of an analogy to argue for a conclusion is known, not surprisingly, as argument by analogy. It is a type of inductive argument that says because two things are alike in some ways, they must be alike in some additional way. For example:

1. Humans feel pain, care for their young, live in social groups, and understand nuclear physics.
2. Apes also feel pain, care for their young, and live in social groups.
3. Therefore, apes can understand nuclear physics.

In argument by analogy, the probability that the conclusion is true depends on the relevant similarities between the two things being compared. The greater the relevant similarities, the more likely the conclusion is true. Humans and apes are relevantly similar in several ways, but the question is, Are they relevantly similar enough to render the conclusion probable? In this case, though humans and apes are similar in some ways, they are not relevantly similar enough to adequately support the conclusion. Humans and apes have many differences—the most relevant of which for this argument is probably in the physiology of their brains and in their capacity for advanced learning.

Arguments by analogy are common in moral reasoning. For example:

1. When a neighbor needs your help (as when he needs to borrow your garden hose to put out a fire in his house), it is morally permissible to lend the neighbor what he needs.
2. Britain is a neighbor of the United States, and it is in dire need of help to win the war against Germany.
3. Therefore, it is morally permissible for the United States to lend Britain the material and equipment it needs to defeat Germany.

This is roughly the moral argument that President Franklin Roosevelt made during World War II to convince Americans to aid Britain in its struggle. The strength of the argument depends on the degree of similarity between the two situations described. At the time, many Americans thought the argument strong.

The fallacy of **faulty analogy** is arguing by an analogy that is weak. In strong arguments by analogy, not only must the degree of similarity be great but also the similarities must be relevant. This means that the similarities must relate specifically to the conclusion. Irrelevant similarities cannot strengthen an argument.

Appeal to Ignorance

This fallacy consists of arguing that the *absence of evidence* entitles us to believe a claim. Consider these two arguments:

- No one has proven that the fetus is not a person, so it is in fact a person.
- It is obviously false that a fetus is a person, because science has not proven that it is a person.

Both these arguments are **appeals to ignorance**. The first one says that because a statement has not been proven false, it must be true. The second one has things the other way around: because a statement has not been proven true, it must be false. The problem with both of these is that a *lack* of evidence cannot be evidence for anything. A dearth of evidence simply indicates that we are ignorant of the facts. If having no evidence could prove something, we could prove all sorts of outrageous claims. We could argue that because no one has proven that there are no space aliens controlling all our moral decisions, there are in fact space aliens controlling all our moral decisions.

Straw Man

Unfortunately, this fallacy is rampant in debates about moral issues. It amounts to misrepresenting someone's claim or argument so it can be more easily refuted. For example, suppose you are trying to argue that a code of ethics for your professional group should be secular so that it can be appreciated and used by as many people as possible, regardless of their religious views. Suppose further that your opponent argues against your claim in this fashion:

> X obviously wants to strip religious faith away from every member of our profession and to banish religion from the realm of ethics. We should not let this happen. We should not let X have her way. Vote against the secular code of ethics.

This argument misrepresents your view, distorting it so that it seems outrageous and unacceptable. Your opponent argues against the distorted version and then concludes that your (original) position should be rejected.

The **straw man** fallacy is not just a bad argument—it flies in the face of the spirit of moral reasoning, which is about seeking understanding through critical thinking and honest and fair exploration of issues. If you wish to be true to the spirit of moral reasoning, then you should not use the straw man fallacy—and you should beware of its use by others.

Appeal to the Person

Appeal to the person (also known as *ad hominem*) is arguing that a claim should be rejected solely because of the characteristics of the person who makes it. Look at these:

- We should reject Alice's assertion that cheating on your taxes is wrong. She's a political libertarian.

- Jerome argues that we should all give a portion of our income to feed the hungry people of the world. But that's just what you'd expect a rich guy like him to say. Ignore him.
- Maria says that animals have rights and that we shouldn't use animal products on moral grounds. Don't believe a word of it. She owns a fur coat—she's a big hypocrite.

In each of these arguments, a claim is rejected on the grounds that the person making it has a particular character, political affiliation, or motive. Such personal characteristics, however, are irrelevant to the truth of a claim. A claim must stand or fall on its own merits. Whether a statement is true or false, it must be judged according to the quality of the reasoning and evidence behind it. Bad people can construct good arguments; good people can construct bad arguments.

Hasty Generalization

Hasty generalization is a fallacy of inductive reasoning. It is the mistake of drawing a conclusion about an entire group of people or things based on an undersized sample of the group.

- In this town three pro-life demonstrators have been arrested for trespassing or assault. I'm telling you, pro-lifers are lawbreakers.
- In the past thirty years, at least two people on death row in this state have been executed and were later found to be innocent by DNA evidence. Why is the state constantly executing innocent people?

In the first argument, a conclusion is drawn about all people with pro-life views from a sample of just three people. When it is spelled out plainly, the leap in logic is clearly preposterous. Yet such preposterous leaps are extremely common. In the second argument, the conclusion is that wrongful executions in the state happen frequently. This conclusion, though, is not justified by the tiny sample of cases.

KEYWORDS

appeal to authority—The fallacy of relying on the opinion of someone thought to be an expert who is not.

appeal to emotion—The fallacy of trying to convince someone to accept a conclusion by appealing only to fear, guilt, anger, hate, compassion, and the like.

appeal to ignorance—The fallacy of arguing that the absence of evidence entitles us to believe a claim.

appeal to the person—The fallacy of arguing that a claim should be rejected solely because of the characteristics of the person who makes it; also known as *ad hominem*.

argument—A group of statements, one of which is supposed to be supported by the rest.

begging the question—The fallacy of arguing in a circle—that is, trying to use a statement as both a premise in an argument and the conclusion of that argument. Such an argument says, in effect, *p* is true because *p* is true.

cogent argument—A strong argument with true premises.

conclusion—The statement supported in an argument.

considered moral judgment—A moral judgment that is as free from bias and distorting passions as possible. We generally trust such a judgment unless there is a reason to doubt it. Examples: "Equals should be treated equally" and "Slavery is wrong."

deductive argument—An argument that is supposed to give logically conclusive support to its conclusion.

equivocation—The fallacy of assigning two different meanings to the same term in an argument.

fallacy—A common but faulty argument.

faulty analogy—The use of a flawed analogy to argue for a conclusion.

hasty generalization—The fallacy of drawing a conclusion about an entire group of people or things based on an undersized sample of the group.

hypothetical syllogism—An argument of the form: If *p*, then *q*; if *q*, then *r*; therefore, if *p*, then *r*.

indicator words—Terms that often appear in arguments to signal the presence of a premise or conclusion, or to indicate that an argument is deductive or inductive.

inductive argument—An argument that is supposed to offer probable support to its conclusion.

invalid argument—A deductive argument that does not offer logically conclusive support for the conclusion.

modus ponens—An argument of the form: If *p*, then *q*; *p*; therefore, *q*.

modus tollens—An argument of the form: If *p*, then *q*; not *q*; therefore, not *p*.

moral statement—A statement affirming that an action is right or wrong or that a person (or one's motive or character) is good or bad.

nonmoral statement—A statement that does not affirm that an action is right or wrong or that a person (or one's motive or character) is good or bad.

premise—A supporting statement in an argument.

slippery slope—The fallacy of using dubious premises to argue that doing a particular action will inevitably lead to other actions that will result in disaster, so you should not do the first action.

sound argument—A valid argument with true premises.

statement—An assertion that something is or is not the case. Also called a *claim*.

straw man—The fallacy of misrepresenting someone's claim or argument so it can be more easily refuted.

strong argument—An inductive argument that provides probable support for its conclusion.

valid argument—A deductive argument that provides logically conclusive support for its conclusion.

weak argument—An inductive argument that does not give probable support to its conclusion.

EXERCISES

Review Questions

1. Are all persuasive arguments valid? Recount a situation in which you tried to persuade someone of a view by using an argument.

2. Can a valid deductive argument ever have false premises?

3. Are the premises of a cogent argument always true? Is the conclusion always true?

4. What is the term designating a valid argument with true premises? a strong argument with true premises?

5. Is the following argument form valid or invalid?

   If p, then q.

   p.

   Therefore, q.

6. Is the following argument form valid or invalid?

   If p, then q.

   If q, then r.

   Therefore, if p, then r.

7. What is the counterexample method?

8. What kind of premises must a moral argument have?

9. What is the best method for evaluating moral premises?
10. Explain the method for locating implied premises.

Essay Questions

1. If moral reasoning is largely about providing good reasons for moral claims, where do feelings enter the picture? Is it possible to present a good argument that you feel strongly about? If so, provide an example of such an argument.
2. Which of the following passages are arguments (in the sense of displaying critical reasoning)? Explain your answers.
   - If you harm someone, that person will harm you.
   - Racial profiling is wrong. It discriminates against racial groups, and discrimination is wrong.
   - If you say something that offends me, I have the right to prevent you from saying it again. After all, words are weapons, and I have a right to prevent the use of weapons against me.
3. What is the difference between persuading someone to believe a claim and giving them reasons to accept it? Can a good argument be persuasive? Why or why not?
4. Why do you think people are tempted to use the straw man fallacy in disagreements on moral issues? How do you feel when someone uses this fallacy against you?
5. What is the appeal to ignorance? Why is it a fallacy?

Argument Exercises

In each of the following arguments, identify the conclusion and premise(s).

1. If John works out at the gym daily, he will be healthier. He is working out at the gym daily. So he will be healthier.
2. If you are no longer a person when you are in a coma, then someone giving you a drug in order to kill you would not be murder. In a coma, you are in fact not a person. Therefore, giving you the drug is not murder.
3. Ghosts do not exist. There is no reliable evidence showing that any disembodied persons exist anywhere.
4. If you smoke, your heart will be damaged. If your heart is damaged, your risk of dying due to heart problems will increase. Therefore, smoking can increase your risk of dying due to heart problems.
5. The mayor is soft on crime. He cut back on misdemeanor enforcement and told the police department to be more lenient on traffic violators.

6. Grow accustomed to the belief that death is nothing to us, because every good and evil lie in sensation. However, death is the deprivation of sensation. Therefore, death is nothing to us.

7. The president is either dishonest or incompetent. He's not incompetent, though, because he's an expert at getting self-serving legislation through Congress. I guess he's just dishonest.

8. Most Republicans are conservatives, and Kurt is a Republican. Therefore, Kurt is probably a conservative. Therefore, Kurt is probably opposed to increases in welfare benefits because most conservatives are opposed to increased welfare benefits.

9. Can people without strong religious beliefs be moral? Countless people have been nonbelievers or nontheists and still behaved according to lofty moral principles (for example, the Buddhists of Asia and the Confucianists of China). Consider also the great secular philosophers from the ancient Greeks to the likes of David Hume and Bertrand Russell. So it is not true that those without strong religious beliefs cannot be moral.

10. Jan is a student at Harvard. No student at Harvard has won a Pulitzer Prize. Therefore, Jan has not won a Pulitzer.

11. We shouldn't pay the lawn-mower guy so much money because he never completes the work, and he will probably just gamble the money away because he has no self-control.

12. Manny, Mo, or Jack crashed the car. Manny couldn't have done it because he was sleeping in his room and was observed the whole time. Mo couldn't have done it because he was out of town at the time and has witnesses to prove it. So the guy who crashed the car had to be Jack.

ETHICAL DILEMMAS

1. Suppose your friend puts forth several arguments in an effort to try to convince you that all abortions are morally wrong. You already have strong views to the contrary, and you know she is a member of an anti-abortion group that advocates violence. In light of these facts, should you dismiss her arguments out of hand? Why or why not? What would constitute a good reason for rejecting her arguments?

2. You believe that all illegal immigrants should be deported. You have no reasons for believing this; you were simply taught to believe it by your parents. Is it morally right for you to adhere to such a view based on no good reasons? Do you have a moral duty to apply critical reasoning to your belief? Why or why not?

3. You argue persuasively for capital punishment, employing the straw man fallacy and hasty generalizations (but no sound or cogent arguments), and you convince your audience. Is it morally permissible for you to use such fallacies to change people's minds? Are you obligated to use at least one sound argument? Explain.

CHAPTER 4

Moral Theories

Whatever else the moral life entails, it surely has moral reasoning at its core. We act, we feel, we choose, and in our best moments, we are guided by the sifting of reasons and the weighing of arguments. Much of the time, we expect—and want—this process to yield plausible moral judgments. We confront the cases that unsettle us and hope to respond to them with credible assessments of the right and the good. In making these judgments, we may appeal to moral standards—principles or rules that help us sort out right and wrong, good and bad. Our deliberations may even work the other way around: moral judgments may help us mold moral principles. If we think carefully about our own deliberations, however, we will likely come to understand that this interplay between moral judgments and principles cannot be the whole story of moral reasoning. From time to time we step back from such considerations and ask ourselves if a trusted moral principle is truly sound, whether a conflict of principles can be resolved, or if a new principle can handle cases that we have never had to address before. When we puzzle over such things, we enter the realm of moral theory. We theorize—trying to use, make, or revise a moral theory or a piece of one.

THEORIES OF RIGHT AND WRONG

A **moral theory** is an explanation of what makes an action right or what makes a person or thing good. Its focus is not the rightness or goodness of specific actions or persons but the very nature of rightness or goodness itself. Moral theories concerned with the goodness of persons or things are known as *theories of value*. Moral theories concerned with the rightness or wrongness of actions are called *theories of obligation*. In this text, we focus mostly on theories of obligation and, unless otherwise indicated, use the more general term *moral theories* to refer to them. A moral theory in this sense, then, is an explanation of what makes an action right or wrong. It says, in effect, that a particular action is right (or wrong) because it has *this* property, or characteristic.

Moral theories and theorizing are hard to avoid. To wonder what makes an action right is to theorize. To try *not* to think much about morality but to rely on your default moral theory—the one you inherited from your family or culture—is of course to live by the lights of a moral theory. To reject all moral theories, to deny the possibility of objective morality, or to embrace a subjectivist view of right and wrong is to have a particular overarching view of morality, a view that in the broadest sense constitutes a moral theory or part of one.

A moral theory provides us with very general norms, or standards, that can help us make sense of our moral experiences, judgments, and principles. (Some moral theories feature only *one* overarching standard.) The standards are meant to be general enough and substantial enough to inform our moral reasoning—to help us assess the worth of less general principles, to shed light on our moral judgments, to corroborate or challenge aspects of our moral experience, and even to generate new lower-level principles if need be.

Moral theories and moral arguments often work together. A statement expressing a moral theory may itself act as the moral premise in an argument. More often, an argument's moral premise is ultimately backed by a moral theory from which the moral premise (principle or rule) is derived. Testing the premise may require examining one or more supporting principles or perhaps the most general norm (the theory) itself.

Classic *utilitarianism* is an example of a simple moral theory, one based on a single, all-encompassing standard: right actions are those that directly produce the greatest overall happiness, everyone considered. What matters most are the consequences of actions. Thus, if there are only two possible actions in a particular situation, and action X produces, say, 100 units of overall happiness for everyone involved (early utilitarians were the first to use this strange-sounding notion of *units* of happiness) while action Y produces only 50 units, action X is the morally right action to perform. The theory therefore identifies what is thought to be the most important factor in the moral life (happiness) and provides a procedure for making judgments about right and wrong actions.

Should we therefore conclude that a moral theory is the final authority in moral reasoning? Not at all. A moral theory is not like a mathematical axiom. From a moral theory we cannot derive in strict logical fashion principles or judgments that will solve all of the problems of our real-world cases. Because moral theories are by definition general and theoretical, they cannot by themselves give us precisely tailored right answers. But neither can we dispense with moral theories and rely solely on judgments about particular cases and issues. In the field of ethics, most philosophers agree that carefully made moral judgments about cases and issues are generally reliable data that we should take very seriously. As mentioned earlier, such opinions are called *considered moral judgments* because they are formed after careful deliberation that is as free of bias as possible. Our considered judgments (including the principles or rules sanctioned by those judgments) by themselves, however, are sometimes of limited use. They may conflict. They may lack sufficient justification. A moral theory provides standards that can help overcome these limitations.

So where does theory fit in our moral deliberations? Theory plays a role along with judgments and principles or rules. In trying to determine the morally right thing to do in a specific case, we may find ourselves reflecting on just one of these elements or on all of them at once. We may, for example, begin by considering the insights embodied in our moral theory, which give some justification to several relevant principles. In light of these principles, we may decide to perform a particular action. But we may also discover that our considered judgment in the case conflicts with the relevant principles or even with the overarching theory. Depending on the weight we give to the particular judgment, we may decide to adjust the principles or the theory so that it is compatible with the judgment. A moral theory can crystallize important insights in morality and thereby give us general guidance as we make judgments about cases and issues. But the judgments—if they are indeed trustworthy—can compel us to reconsider the theory.

The ultimate goal in this give-and-take of theory and judgment (or principle) is a kind of close coherence between the two—what has come to be known as *reflective equilibrium*.[1] They should fit together as closely as possible, with maximum agreement between them. This process is similar to the one used in science to reconcile theory and experimental data, a topic we address in more detail later in this chapter.

MAJOR THEORIES

Moral philosophers have traditionally grouped theories of morality into two major categories: consequentialist (or teleological) and nonconsequentialist (or deontological). In general, **consequentialist** moral theories say that what makes an action right is its *consequences*. Specifically, the rightness of an action depends on the amount of good it produces. A consequentialist theory may define the good in different ways—as, for example, pleasure, happiness, well-being, flourishing, or knowledge. But however good is defined, the morally right action is the one that results in the most favorable balance of good over bad.

Nonconsequentialist moral theories say that the rightness of an action does *not* depend entirely on its consequences. It depends primarily, or completely, on the nature of the action itself. To a nonconsequentialist, the balance of good over bad that results from an action may matter little or not at all. What is of primary concern is the *kind* of action in question. To a consequentialist, telling a lie may be considered wrong because it leads to more unhappiness than other actions do. To a nonconsequentialist, telling a lie may be considered wrong simply because it violates an exceptionless rule. Thus, by nonconsequentialist lights, an action could be morally right even though it produces less good than any alternative action.

Consequentialist Theories

There are several consequentialist (teleological) theories, each differing on who is to benefit from the goods or what kinds of goods are to be pursued. But two theories have received the most attention from moral philosophers: utilitarianism and ethical egoism.

Utilitarianism says that the morally right action is the one that produces the most favorable balance of good over evil, everyone considered. That is, the right action maximizes the good (however *good* is defined) better than any alternative action, everyone considered. Utilitarianism insists that *everyone* affected by an action must be included in any proper calculation of overall consequences. The crucial factor is how much net good is produced when everyone involved is counted.

Moral philosophers distinguish two major types of utilitarianism, according to whether judgments of rightness focus on individual acts (without reference to rules) or on rules that cover various categories of acts. **Act-utilitarianism** says that right actions are those that *directly* produce the greatest overall good, everyone considered. The consequences that flow directly from a particular act are all that matter; rules are irrelevant to this calculation. In act-utilitarianism, each situation calling for a moral judgment is unique and demands a new calculation of the balance of good over evil. Thus, breaking a promise may be right in one situation and wrong in another, depending on the consequences. **Rule-utilitarianism,** on the other hand, says that the morally right action is the one *covered by a rule* that if generally followed would produce the most favorable balance of good over evil, everyone considered. The consequences of generally following a rule are of supreme importance—not the direct consequences of performing a particular action. Specific rules are justified because if people follow them all of the time (or most of the time), the result will be a general maximization of good over evil. We are to follow such rules consistently even if doing so in a particular circumstance results in bad consequences.

Ethical egoism says that the morally right action is the one that produces the most favorable balance of good over evil *for oneself*. That is, in every situation the right action is the one that advances one's own best interests. In each circumstance, the ethical egoist must ask, Which action, among all possible actions, will result in the most good *for me*? Ironically, it may be possible for an ethical egoist to consistently practice this creed without appearing to be selfish or committing many selfishly unkind acts. The egoist may think that *completely* disregarding the welfare of others is not in his or her best interests. After all, people tend to resent such behavior and may respond accordingly. Nevertheless, the bottom line in all moral deliberations is whether an action maximizes the good for the egoist. This approach to morality seems to radically conflict with commonsense moral experience as well as with the basic principles of most other moral theories.

Nonconsequentialist Theories

Nonconsequentialist (deontological) theories also take various forms. They differ on, among other things, the number of foundational principles or basic rules used and the ultimate basis of those principles.

By far the most influential nonconsequentialist theory is that of Immanuel Kant (1724–1804). Kant wanted to establish as the foundation of his theory a single principle from which all additional maxims can be derived, a principle he called the **categorical imperative**. One way that he states his principle is "Act only on that maxim through which you can at the same time will that it should become a universal law."[2] (Kant insists that he formulates just one principle but expresses it in several different forms; the forms, however, seem to be separate principles.) The categorical imperative, Kant says, is self-evident—and therefore founded on reason. The principle and the maxims derived from it are also universal (applying to all persons) and absolutist, meaning that they are moral laws that have no exceptions. **Kant's theory**, then, is the view that the morally right action is the one done in accordance with the categorical imperative.

For Kant, every action implies a rule or maxim that says, in effect, always do this in these circumstances. An action is right, he says, if and only if you could rationally will the rule to be universal—to have everyone in a similar situation always act according to the same rule. Breaking promises is wrong because if the implied rule (something like "Break promises whenever you want") were universalized (if everyone followed the rule), then no promise anywhere could be trusted and the whole convention of promise making would be obliterated—and no one would be willing to live in such a world. In other words, universalizing the breaking of promises would result in a logically contradictory state of affairs, a situation that makes no moral sense.

Notice again the stark contrast between utilitarianism and Kant's theory. For the former, the rightness of an action depends solely on its consequences, on what results the action produces for the individuals involved. For the latter, the consequences of actions for particular individuals never enter into the equation. An action is right if and only if it possesses a particular property—the property of according with the categorical imperative, of not involving a logical contradiction.

Another notable nonconsequentialist view is the theory of natural law. **Natural law theory** says that the morally right action is the one that follows the dictates of nature. What does nature have to do with ethics? According to the most influential form of this theory (traditional natural law theory), the natural world, including humankind, exhibits a rational order in which everything has its proper place and purpose, with each thing given a specific role to play by God. In this grand order, natural laws reflect how the world is as well as how it should be. People are supposed to live according to natural law—that is, they are to fulfill their rightful, *natural* purpose. To act morally, they must act naturally; they must do what they were designed to do by God. They must obey the absolutist moral rules that anyone can read in the natural order.

A natural law theorist might reason like this: Lying is immoral because it goes against human nature. Truth telling is natural for humans because they are social creatures with an inborn tendency to care about the welfare of others. Truth telling helps humans get along, maintain viable societies, and show respect for others. Lying is therefore unnatural and wrong. Another example: Some natural law theorists claim that "unnatural" sexual activity is immoral. They argue that because the natural purpose of sex is procreation, and such practices as homosexual behavior or anal sex have nothing to do with procreation, these practices are immoral.

Another critical aspect of the traditional theory is that it insists that humans can discover what is natural, and thus moral, through reason. God has created a natural order and given humans the gift of rationality to correctly apprehend this order. This means that any rational person—whether religious or not—can discern the moral rules and live a moral life.

One of the simplest nonconsequentialist theories is the divine command theory. It says that the morally right action is the one that God commands. An action is right if and only if God says it is. The rightness of an action does not depend in any way on its consequences. According to the divine command theory, an action may be deemed right even though it does *not* maximize the good, or deemed wrong even if it does maximize the good. It may incorporate one principle only (the core principle that God makes rightness) or the core principle plus several subordinate rules, as is the case with divine command views that designate the Ten Commandments as a God-made moral code.

EVALUATING THEORIES

We come now to the question that moral philosophers have been asking in one way or another for centuries: Is this moral theory a *good* theory? That is, Is it true? Does it reliably explain what makes an action right? As we have seen, not all moral theories are created equal. Some are better than others; some are seriously flawed; and some, though imperfect, have taught the world important lessons about the moral life.

The next question, of course, is, How do we go about answering the first question? At first glance, it seems that impartially judging the worth of a moral theory is impossible, since we all look at the world through our own tainted lens, our own moral theory or theory fragments. Our earlier review of subjectivism and relativism, however, suggests that this worry is overblown. More to the point, there are plausible criteria that we can use to evaluate the adequacy of moral theories (our own and those of others), standards that moral philosophers and others have used to appraise even the most complex theories of morality. These are what we may call the *moral criteria of adequacy*.

The first step in any theory assessment (before using these criteria) is to ensure that the theory meets the minimum requirement of *coherence*. A moral theory that is coherent is *eligible* to be evaluated using the criteria of adequacy. A coherent theory is internally consistent, which means that its central claims are consistent with each other—they are not contradictory. An internally consistent theory would not assert, for example, both that (1) actions are right if and only if they are natural and (2) it is morally right to use unnatural means to save a life. Contradictory claims assert both that something *is* and *is not* the case; one statement says X and another says not-X. When claims conflict in this way, we know that at least one of them is false. So if two substantial claims in a theory are contradictory, one of the claims must be false—and the theory is refuted. This kind of inconsistency is such a serious shortcoming in a moral theory that further evaluation of it would be unnecessary. It is, in fact, not eligible for evaluation. Ineligible theories would get low marks on each criterion of adequacy.

Eligible moral theories are a different matter. Unlike ineligible theories, they are not guaranteed to fare poorly when evaluated, and testing their mettle with the moral criteria of adequacy is almost always revealing. But how do we use these criteria? The answer is that we apply them in much the same way and for a few of the same reasons that scientists apply their criteria to scientific theories.

Scientific theories are introduced to explain data concerning the causes of events—why something happens as it does or why it is the way it is. Usually scientists devise several theories (explanations) of a phenomenon, ensuring that each one is minimally adequate for evaluation. Then they try to determine which of these offers the best explanation for the data in question, for they know that the best theory is the one most likely to be true. To discover which one is the best, they must judge each theory according to some generally accepted standards—the scientific criteria of adequacy. One criterion, for example, is *conservatism*: how well a theory fits with what scientists already know. A scientific theory that conflicts with existing knowledge (well-established facts, scientific laws, or extensively confirmed theories) is not likely to be true. The more conservative a theory is (that is, the less it conflicts with existing knowledge), the more likely it is to be true. All things being equal, a conservative theory is better than one that is not conservative. Another criterion is *fruitfulness*: how many successful novel predictions the theory makes. The more such predictions, the more plausible the theory is.

Now consider the following three criteria of adequacy for moral theories.

Criterion 1: Consistency with Considered Judgments

To be worth evaluating, a plausible scientific theory must be consistent with the data it was introduced to explain. A theory meant to explain an epidemic, for example, must account for the nature of the disease and the method of transmission. Otherwise it is a very poor theory. A moral theory must also be consistent with the data it was introduced to explain. A moral theory is supposed to explain what makes an action right, and the data relevant to that issue are our *considered moral judgments*.

Recall that considered moral judgments are views that we form after careful deliberation under conditions that minimize bias and error. They are therefore thought to have considerable weight as reasons or evidence in moral matters, even though they can be mistaken and other considerations (such as an established moral principle or a well-supported theory) can sometimes overrule them.

A moral theory that is inconsistent with trustworthy judgments is at least dubious and likely to be false, and in need of drastic overhaul or rejection. There is something seriously wrong, for example, with a theory that approves of the murder of innocent people, the wanton torture of children, or the enslavement of millions of men and women. As we will see in the next chapter, inconsistency with considered judgments can be the undoing of even the most influential and attractive moral theories.

Consider theory X. It says that right actions are those that enhance the harmonious functioning of a community. On the face of it, this theory appears to be a wise policy. But it seems to imply that certain heinous acts are right. It suggests, for example, that if killing an innocent person would enhance a community's harmonious functioning, killing that person would be right. This view conflicts dramatically with our considered judgment that murdering an innocent person just to make a community happy is wrong. Theory X should be rejected.

Criterion 2: Consistency with Our Moral Experience

As we saw earlier, a good scientific theory should be conservative. It should, in other words, be consistent with scientific background knowledge—with the many beliefs that science has already firmly established. Likewise, a plausible moral theory should be consistent with moral background knowledge—with what we take to be the fundamental facts of our moral experience. Whatever our views on morality, few of us would deny that we do in fact have these experiences:

- We sometimes make moral judgments.
- We often give reasons for particular moral beliefs.
- We are sometimes mistaken in our moral beliefs.
- We occasionally have moral disagreements.
- We occasionally commit wrongful acts.

As is the case with theories that conflict with considered judgments, a theory in conflict with these experiences is at least dubious and probably false. A moral theory is inconsistent with the moral life if it implies that we do not have one or more of these basic moral experiences.

Suppose theory Y says that our feelings alone determine whether actions are right. If our feelings lead us to believe that an action is right, then it is right. But this theory suggests that we are *never* mistaken in our moral beliefs, for if our feelings determine what is right, we cannot be wrong. Whatever we happen to feel tells us what actions are right. Our moral experience, however, is good evidence that we are *not* morally infallible. Theory Y therefore is problematic, to say the least.

Could we possibly be mistaken about our moral experience? Yes. It is possible that our experience of the moral life is illusory. Perhaps we are morally infallible after all, or maybe we do not actually make moral judgments. But like our considered moral judgments, our common-sense moral experience carries weight as evidence—good evidence that the moral life is, for the most part, as we think it is. We therefore are entitled to accept this evidence as trustworthy unless we have good reason to think otherwise.

Criterion 3: Usefulness in Moral Problem Solving

Good scientific theories increase our understanding of the world, and greater understanding leads to greater usefulness—the capacity to solve problems and answer questions. The more useful a scientific theory is, the more credibility it acquires. A good moral theory is also useful—it helps us solve moral problems in real-life situations. It helps us make reliable judgments about moral principles and actions and resolve conflicts among conflicting judgments, principles, and the theory itself. A major reason for devising a moral theory is to obtain this kind of practical guidance.

Usefulness is a necessary, though not sufficient, characteristic of a good moral theory. This means that all good theories are useful, but usefulness alone does not make a moral theory good. It is possible for a bad theory to be useful as well (to be useful but fail some other criterion of adequacy). But any moral theory that lacks usefulness is a dubious theory.

Now we can be more specific about the similarities between science and ethics in handling theory and data. In science, the interaction between a theory and the relevant data is dynamic. The theory is designed to explain the data, so the data help shape the theory. But a plausible theory can give scientists good reasons to accept or reject specific data or to reinterpret them. Both the theory and the data contribute to the process of searching for the truth. Scientists work to get the balance between these two just right. They try to ensure a very close fit between them—so close that there is no need for major alterations in either the theory or the data. In ethics, the link between theory and data (considered judgments) is similar. Considered judgments help shape theory (and its principles or rules), and a good theory sheds light on judgments and helps adjudicate conflicts between judgments and other moral statements. As in science, we should strive for a strong logical harmony between theory, data, and subordinate principles.

Remember, though, theory evaluation is not a mechanical process, and neither is the application of theories to moral problems. There is no formula or set of instructions for applying our three criteria to a theory. Neither is there a calculating machine for determining how much weight to give each criterion in particular situations. We must make an informed judgment about the importance of particular criteria in each new instance. Nevertheless, applying the criteria is not a subjective, arbitrary affair. It is rational and objective—such as, for example, the diagnosis of an illness, based on the educated judgment of a physician using appropriate guidelines.

Now suppose you apply the moral criteria of adequacy and reach a verdict on the worth of a theory: you reject it. Should this verdict be the end of your inquiry? In general, no. There is often much to be learned from even seriously defective theories. Many philosophers who reject utilitarianism, for example, also believe that it makes a valuable point that any theory should take into account: the consequences of actions do matter. Judiciously applying the criteria of adequacy to a theory can help us see a theory's strengths as well as its weaknesses. Such insights can inspire us to improve any moral theory, or perhaps create a new one.

You will get a chance to see firsthand how theory evaluation is done. In the chapters that follow, we will apply the moral criteria of adequacy to several major moral theories.

KEYWORDS

act-utilitarianism—The theory that morally right actions are those that directly produce the greatest overall good, everyone considered.

categorical imperative—A command that we should follow regardless of our particular wants and needs; also, the single principle that defines Kant's ethical system, from which all additional maxims can be derived.

consequentialist theory—A moral theory asserting that what makes an action right is its consequences.

ethical egoism—The theory that the morally right action is the one that advances one's own best interests.

Kant's theory—A theory asserting that the morally right action is the one done in accordance with the categorical imperative.

moral theory—An explanation of what makes an action right or what makes a person or thing good.

natural law theory—A theory asserting that the morally right action is the one that follows the dictates of nature.

nonconsequentialist theory—A moral theory asserting that the rightness of an action does not depend on its consequences.

rule-utilitarianism—The theory that the morally right action is the one covered by a rule that if generally followed would produce the most favorable balance of good over evil, everyone considered.

utilitarianism—A theory asserting that the morally right action is the one that produces the most favorable balance of good over evil, everyone considered.

EXERCISES

Review Questions

1. Is a moral theory the final authority in moral reasoning? Why or why not?
2. In moral reasoning, what is the relationship between moral theories and moral judgments or principles?
3. How can a moral theory be used in a moral argument?
4. Do philosophers generally think we should trust our considered moral judgments? Can our considered moral judgments be mistaken?
5. What is Kant's main complaint against consequentialist theories?
6. Define the two forms of utilitarianism.
7. According to Kant's moral theory, what makes an action right?
8. What are the three moral criteria of adequacy?
9. Name two nonconsequentialist theories.
10. Name three common moral experiences that we all have.

Essay Questions

1. Do you try to guide your moral choices with a moral code or a moral theory, or both? If so, how?
2. Suppose you try to use the Ten Commandments as a moral code to help you make moral decisions. How would you resolve conflicts between commandments? Does your approach to resolving the conflicts imply a moral theory? If so, can you explain the main idea behind the theory?
3. What considered moral judgments have you made or appealed to in the past month? Do you think that these judgments are reflective of a moral principle or moral theory you implicitly appeal to? If so, what is it?
4. Would you describe your approach to morality as consequentialist, nonconsequentialist, or some combination of both? What reasons do you have for adopting this particular approach?

5. Give an example of a possible conflict between a consequentialist theory and a considered moral judgment. (Show how these two may be inconsistent.)

6. Provide an example of a conflict between a nonconsequentialist theory and a moral judgment based on the consequences of an action.

7. Using the moral criteria of adequacy, evaluate act-utilitarianism.

8. Using the moral criteria of adequacy, evaluate natural law theory.

ETHICAL DILEMMAS

1. Suppose you are an act-utilitarian, and you must choose between two courses of action. In the first action, you could make a stranger very happy by giving her $100. In the second action, you could make another stranger even happier by giving him the same amount of money—but this action would involve breaking a promise to a friend. According to act-utilitarianism, which action is the morally right one? Do you agree with this choice? Why or why not?

2. Imagine that your preferred moral theory implies that racial discrimination is morally permissible—an implication that is in direct conflict with your considered moral judgments. Would such a conflict suggest to you that the theory must be defective? Why or why not?

3. Suppose your preferred moral theory is based entirely on love—that is, you believe that right actions are those that issue from a feeling of empathy, compassion, or mercy. Now imagine that a homeless man assaults you and steals your wallet, and then you see him do the same thing to two other people. How would your love theory apply to this case? Would there be a conflict between love and the principle of justice or the community's moral standards? Would your theory lead you to go against your considered moral judgments? Assess the worth of the love theory.

Endnotes

1. John Rawls, *A Theory of Justice*, rev. ed. (Cambridge, MA: Harvard University Press, Belknap Press, 1999).

2. Immanuel Kant, *Groundwork of the Metaphysic of Morals,* trans. H. J. Paton (1948; reprint, New York: Harper & Row, 1964), 88.

CHAPTER 5

Ethical Egoism

There is something in consequentialist moral theories that we find appealing, something simple and commonsensical that jibes with everyday moral experience. This attractive core is the notion that right actions must produce the best balance of good over evil. Never mind (for now) how *good* and *evil* are defined. The essential concern is how much good can result from actions performed. In this chapter, we examine the plausibility of this consequentialist maxim and explore how it is worked out in one of its most debated theories: ethical egoism. In the next chapter we will conduct the same kind of examination of the most influential consequentialist theory: utilitarianism.

Ethical egoism is the theory that the right action is the one that advances one's own best interests. It is a provocative doctrine, in part because it forces us to consider two opposing attitudes in ourselves. On the one hand, we tend to view selfish or flagrantly self-interested behavior as wicked, or at least troubling. Self-love is bad love. We frown on people who trample others in life to get ahead. On the other hand, sometimes we want to look out for number one, to give priority to our own needs and desires. We think, If we do not help ourselves, who will? Self-love is good love.

Ethical egoism says that one's only moral duty is to promote the most favorable balance of good over evil for oneself. Each person must put his or her own welfare first. Advancing the interests of others is part of this moral equation only if it helps promote one's own good. Yet this extreme self-interest is not necessarily selfishness. Selfish acts advance one's own interests regardless of how others are affected. Self-interested acts promote one's own interests but not necessarily to the detriment of others. To further your own interests you may actually find yourself helping others. To gain some advantage, you may perform actions that are decidedly unselfish.

Just as we cannot equate ethical egoism with selfishness, neither can we assume it is synonymous with self-indulgence or recklessness. An ethical egoist does not necessarily do whatever she desires to do or whatever gives her the most immediate pleasure. She does what is in her best interests, and instant gratification may not be in her best interests. She may want to spend all of her money at the casino or work eighteen hours a day, but over the long haul doing so may be disastrous for her. Even ethical egoists have to consider the long-term effects of their actions. They also have to take into account their interactions with others. At least most of the time, egoists are probably better off if they cooperate with others, develop reciprocal relationships, and avoid actions that antagonize people in their community or society.

Ethical egoism comes in two forms: one applies the doctrine to individual *acts* and one to relevant *rules*. **Act-egoism** says that to determine right action, you must apply the egoistic principle to individual acts. Act A is preferable to act B because it promotes your self-interest better. **Rule-egoism** says that to determine right action, you must see if an act falls under a rule that if consistently followed would maximize your self-interest. Act A is preferable to act B because it falls under a rule that maximizes your self-interest better than any other relevant rule applying to act B. An ethical egoist can define self-interest in various ways. The Greek philosopher Epicurus (341–270 B.C.E.), a famous ethical egoist from whose name we derive the words *epicure* and *epicurean*, gave a hedonist answer: The greatest good is pleasure, and the greatest evil, pain. The duty of a good ethical egoist is to maximize pleasure for oneself. (Contrary to legend, Epicurus thought that wanton overindulgence in the delights of the senses was not in one's best interests. He insisted that the best pleasures were those of the contemplative life and that extravagant pleasures such as drunkenness and gluttony eventually lead to misery.) Other egoistic notions of the greatest good include self-actualization (fulfilling one's potential), security and material success, satisfaction of desires, acquisition of power, and the experience of happiness.

To many people, ethical egoism may sound alien, especially if they have heard all their lives about the noble virtue of altruism and the evils of self-centeredness. But consider that self-interest is a pillar on which the economic system of capitalism is built. In a capitalist system, self-interest is supposed to drive people to seek advantages for themselves in the marketplace, compelling them to compete against each other to build a better mousetrap at a lower price. Economists argue that the result of this clash of self-interests is a better, more prosperous society.

APPLYING THE THEORY

Suppose Rosa is a successful executive at a large media corporation, and she has her eye on a vice president's position, which has just become vacant. Vincent, another successful executive in the company, also wants the VP job. Management wants to fill the vacancy as soon as possible, and they are trying to decide between the two most qualified candidates—Rosa and Vincent. One day Rosa discovers some documents left near a photocopier and quickly realizes that they belong to Vincent. One of them is an old memo from the president of a company where Vincent used to work. In it, the president lambastes Vincent for botching an important company project. Rosa knows that despite the content of the memo, Vincent has had an exemplary professional career in which he has managed most of his projects extremely well. In fact, she believes that the two of them are about equal in professional skills and accomplishments. She also knows that if management saw the memo, they would almost certainly choose her over Vincent for the VP position. She figures that Vincent probably left the documents there by mistake and would soon return to retrieve them. Impulsively, she makes a copy of the memo for herself.

Now she is confronted with a moral choice. Let us suppose that she has only three options. First, she can destroy her copy of the memo and forget about the whole incident. Second, she can discredit Vincent by showing it to management, thereby securing the VP slot for herself. Third, she can achieve the same result by discrediting Vincent surreptitiously: she can simply leave a copy where management is sure to discover it. Let us also assume that she is an act-egoist who defines her self-interest as self-actualization. Self-actualization for her means developing into the most powerful, most highly respected executive in her profession while maximizing the virtues of loyalty and honesty.

So by the lights of her act-egoism what should Rosa do? Which choice is in her best interests? Option one is neutral regarding her self-interest. If she destroys her copy of the memo, she will neither gain nor lose an advantage for herself. Option two is more complicated. If she overtly discredits Vincent, she will probably land the VP spot—a feat that fits nicely with her desire to become a powerful executive. But such a barefaced sabotaging of someone else's career would likely trouble management, and their loss of some respect for Rosa would impede future advancement in her career. They may also come to distrust her. Rosa's backstabbing would also probably erode the trust and respect of her subordinates (those who report to her). If so, their performance may suffer, and any deficiencies in Rosa's subordinates would reflect on her leadership skills. Over time, she may be able to regain the respect of management through dazzling successes in her field, but the respect and trust of others may be much harder to regain. Option two involves the unauthorized, deceitful use of personal information against another person—not an action that encourages the virtue of honesty in Rosa. In fact, her dishonesty may weaken her moral resolve and make similar acts of deceit more probable.

Like option two, option three would likely secure the VP job for Rosa. But because the deed is surreptitious, it would probably not diminish the respect and trust of others. There is a probability, however, that Rosa's secret would eventually be uncovered—especially if Vincent suspects Rosa, which is likely. If she is found out, the damage done to her reputation (and possibly her career) might be greater than that caused by the more up-front tack of option two. Also like option two, option three might weaken the virtue of honesty in Rosa's character.

Given this situation and Rosa's brand of act-egoism, she should probably go with option three—but only if the risk of being found out is extremely low. Option three promotes her self-interest dramatically by securing the coveted job at a relatively low cost (a possible erosion of virtue). Option two would also land the job but at very high cost—a loss of other people's trust and respect, a possible decrease in her chances for career advancement, damage to her professional reputation, and a likely lessening of a virtue critical to Rosa's self-actualization (honesty).

If Rosa believes that the risks to her career and character involved in options two and three are too high, she should probably choose option one. This choice would not promote her best interests, but it would not diminish them either.

Would Rosa's action be any different if judged from the perspective of rule-egoism? Suppose Rosa, like many other ethical egoists, thinks that her actions should be guided by this rule (or something like it): "People should be honest in their dealings with others—that is, except in insignificant matters (white lies), they should not lie to others or mislead them." She believes that adhering to this prohibition against dishonesty is in her best interests. The rule, however, would disallow both options two and three, for they involve significant deception. Only option one would be left. But if obeying the rule would lead to a major setback for her interests, Rosa might decide to ignore it in this case (or reject it altogether as contrary to the spirit of ethical egoism). If so, she might have to fall back to act-egoism and decide in favor of option three.

EVALUATING THE THEORY

Is ethical egoism a plausible moral theory? Let us find out by examining arguments in its favor and applying the moral criteria of adequacy.

The primary argument for ethical egoism depends heavily on a scientific theory known as **psychological egoism,** the view that the motive for all our actions is self-interest. Whatever we do, we do because we want to promote our own welfare. Psychological egoism, we are told, is simply a description of the true nature of our motivations. We are, in short, born to look out for number one.

Putting psychological egoism to good use, the ethical egoist reasons as follows: We can never be morally obligated to perform an action that we cannot possibly do. This is just an obvious fact about morality. Because we are *not able* to prevent a hurricane from blasting across a coastal city, we are *not morally obligated* to prevent it. Likewise, because we are not able to perform an action except out of self-interest (the claim of psychological egoism), we are not morally obligated to perform an action unless motivated by self-interest. That is, we are morally obligated to do only what our self-interest motivates us to do. Here is the argument stated more formally:

1. We are not able to perform an action except out of self-interest (psychological egoism).

2. We are not morally obligated to perform an action unless motivated by self-interest.

3. Therefore, we are morally obligated to do only what our self-interest motivates us to do.

Notice that even if psychological egoism is true, this argument does not establish that an action is right if and only if it promotes one's self-interest (the claim of ethical egoism). But it does demonstrate that an action cannot be right unless it at least promotes one's self-interest. To put it another way, an action that does not advance one's own welfare cannot be right.

Is psychological egoism true? Many people think it is and offer several arguments in its favor. One line of reasoning is that psychological egoism is true because experience shows that all our actions are in fact motivated by self-interest. All our actions—including seemingly altruistic ones—are performed to gain some benefit for ourselves. This argument, however, is far from conclusive. Sometimes people do perform altruistic acts because doing so is in their best interests. One person may contribute to charity because such generosity furthers his political ambitions. Another person may do volunteer work for the Red Cross because it looks good on her résumé. But people also seem to do things that are *not* motivated by self-interest. A person may risk his life by rushing into a burning building to rescue a complete stranger. Another may impair her health by donating a kidney to prevent one of her children from dying. Explanations that appeal to self-interest in such cases seem implausible. Moreover, people often have self-destructive habits (for example, drinking excessively and driving recklessly)—habits that are unlikely to be in anyone's best interests.

Some ethical egoists may argue in a slightly different vein: People get satisfaction (or happiness or pleasure) from what they do, including their so-called unselfish or altruistic acts. Therefore, they perform unselfish or altruistic actions because doing so gives them satisfaction. A man saves a child from a burning building because he wants the emotional satisfaction that comes from saving a life. Our actions, no matter how we characterize them, are all about self-interest.

This argument is based on a conceptual confusion. It says that we perform selfless acts to achieve satisfaction. Satisfaction is the object of the whole exercise. But if we experience satisfaction in performing an action, that does not show that our goal in performing the action is satisfaction. A much more plausible account is that we desire something other than satisfaction and then experience satisfaction as a result of getting what we desired. Consider, for example, our man who saves the child from a fire. He rescues the child and feels satisfaction—but he could not have experienced that satisfaction unless he already had a desire to save the child or cared what happened to her. If he did not have such a desire or care about her, how could he have derived any satisfaction from his actions? To experience satisfaction he had to have a desire for something other than his own satisfaction. The moral of the story is that satisfaction is the result of getting what we want—not the object of our desires.

This view fits well with our own experience. Most often when we act according to some purpose, we are not focused on, or aware of, our satisfaction. We concentrate on obtaining the real object of our efforts, and when we succeed, we then feel satisfaction.

The philosopher Joel Feinberg makes a similar point about the pursuit of happiness. He asks us to imagine a person, Jones, who has no desire for much of anything—except happiness. Jones has no interest in knowledge for its own sake, the beauty of nature, art and literature, sports, crafts, or business. But Jones does have "an overwhelming passion for, a complete preoccupation with, his own happiness. The one desire of his life is to be happy."[1] The irony is that using this approach, Jones will *not* find happiness. He cannot pursue happiness directly and expect to find it. To achieve happiness, he must pursue other aims whose pursuit yields happiness as a by-product. We must conclude that it is not the case that our only motivation for our actions is the desire for happiness (or satisfaction or pleasure).

These reflections show that psychological egoism is a dubious theory, and if we construe self-interest as satisfaction, pleasure, or happiness, the theory seems false. Still, some may not give up the argument from experience (mentioned earlier), insisting that when properly interpreted, all our actions (including those that seem purely altruistic or unselfish) can be shown to be motivated by self-interest. All of the counterexamples that seem to suggest that psychological egoism is false actually are evidence that it is true. A donor's contributions to a charity may seem altruistic, but he is really trying to impress a woman he would like to date. A volunteer's work at the Red Cross may seem unselfish, but she is just trying to cultivate some business contacts. Every counterexample can be reinterpreted to support the theory.

Critics have been quick to charge that this way of defending psychological egoism is a mistake. It renders the theory untestable and useless. It ensures that no evidence could possibly count against it, and therefore it does not tell us anything about self-interested actions. Anything we say about such actions would be consistent with the theory. Any theory that is so uninformative could not be used to support another theory—including ethical egoism.

So far we have found the arguments for ethical egoism ineffective. Now we can ask another question: Are there any good arguments *against* ethical egoism? This is where the moral criteria of adequacy come in.

Recall that an important first step in evaluating a moral theory (or any other kind of theory) is to determine if it meets the minimum requirement of coherence, or internal consistency. As it turns out, some critics of ethical egoism have brought the charge of logical or practical inconsistency against the theory. But in general these criticisms seem to fall short of a knockout blow to ethical egoism. Devising counterarguments that can undercut the criticisms seems to be a straightforward business. Let us assume, then, that ethical egoism is in fact eligible for evaluation using the criteria of adequacy.

We begin with Criterion 1, consistency with considered judgments. A major criticism of ethical egoism is that it is *not* consistent with many of our considered moral judgments—judgments that seem highly plausible and commonsensical. Specifically, ethical egoism seems to sanction actions that we would surely regard as abominable. Suppose a young man visits his elderly, bedridden father. When he sees that no one else is around, he uses a pillow to smother the old man in order to collect on his life insurance. Suppose also that the action is in the son's best interests; it will cause not the least bit of unpleasant feelings in him; and the crime will remain his own terrible secret. According to ethical egoism, this heinous act is morally right. The son did his duty.

An ethical egoist might object to this line by saying that *refraining* from committing evil acts is actually endorsed by ethical egoism—one's best interests are served by refraining. You should not murder or steal, for example, because it might encourage others to do the same to you, or it might undermine trust, security, or cooperation in society, which would not be in your best interests. For these reasons, you should obey the law or the rules of conventional morality (as the rule-egoist might do).

But following the rules is clearly not always in one's best interests. Sometimes committing a wicked act really does promote one's own welfare. In the case of the murdering son, no one will seek revenge for the secret murder, cooperation and trust in society will not be affected, and the murderer will suffer no psychological torments. There seems to be no downside here—but the son's rewards for committing the deed will be great. Consistently looking out for one's own welfare sometimes requires rule violations and exceptions. In fact, some argue that the interests of ethical egoists may be best served when they urge everyone else to obey the rules while they themselves secretly break them.

If ethical egoism does conflict with our considered judgments, it is questionable at best. But it has been accused of another defect as well: it fails Criterion 2, consistency with our moral experiences.

One aspect of morality is so fundamental that we may plausibly view it as a basic fact of the moral life: moral impartiality, or treating equals equally. We know that in our dealings with the world, we are supposed to take into account the treatment of others as well as that of ourselves. The moral life is lived with the wider world in mind. We must give all persons their due and treat all equals equally, for in the moral sense we are all equals. Each person is presumed to have the same rights as everyone else—and to have interests that are just as important as everyone else's—unless we have good reason for thinking otherwise. If one person is qualified for a job, and another person is equally qualified, we would be guilty of discrimination if we hired one and not the other based solely on race, sex, skin color, or ancestry (this is so because these factors are not morally relevant). People who do treat equals unequally in such ways are known as racists, sexists, bigots, and the like. Probably the most serious charge against ethical egoism is that it discriminates against people in the same fashion. It arbitrarily treats the interests of some people (oneself) as more important than the interests of all others (the rest of the world)—even though there is no morally relevant difference between the two.

The failure of ethical egoism to treat equals equally seems a serious defect in the theory. It conflicts with a major component of our moral existence. For many critics, this single defect is enough reason to reject the theory.

Recall that Criterion 3 is usefulness in moral problem solving. Some philosophers argue that ethical egoism fails this standard because the theory seems to lead to contradictory advice or conflicting actions. If real, this problem would constitute a significant failing of the theory. But these criticisms depend on controversial assumptions about ethical egoism or morality in general, so we will not dwell on them here.

Our analysis of ethical egoism's problems using the first t\
should be sufficient to raise serious doubts about the theory

KEYWORDS

act-egoism—The theory that to determine right action, you must apply the egoistic principle to individual acts.

psychological egoism—The scientific view that the motive for all our actions is self-interest.

rule-egoism—The theory that to determine right action, you must see if an act falls under a rule that if consistently followed would maximize your self-interest.

EXERCISES

Review Questions

1. What is the difference between act-egoism and rule-egoism?
2. If psychological egoism were true, would this fact show that ethical egoism must be true?
3. What is the psychological egoist argument for ethical egoism?
4. Is psychological egoism true? Why or why not?
5. In what way is ethical egoism not consistent with our considered moral judgments?
6. Why do critics regard ethical egoism as an inadequate moral theory?
7. How does ethical egoism seem to conflict with the principle of impartiality?
8. Does ethical egoism imply an unrestrained pursuit of pleasure?
9. What is the difference between self-interest and selfishness?
10. How does self-interest operate in capitalist economies?

ETHICAL DILEMMAS

Explain how ethical egoism (act-egoism or rule-egoism) could be applied in the following scenarios to determine the proper course of action.

1. Your best friend is on trial for murder, and only your testimony can show that she is innocent. But if you testify, you will incriminate yourself, and incriminating yourself will likely lead to a lifetime prison sentence for you. If you say nothing, you will avoid prison and any other legal punishment. Your friend, however, will almost certainly get the death penalty. Should you testify?

2. You are a person of modest means who has been asked to contribute $1,000 to help feed the poor and hungry in Africa. Giving less than that will accomplish nothing. If you contribute that much money, thirty hungry people will survive for a full year, but you will not be able to afford dental work to alleviate the severe pain in your teeth. Giving or not giving the money are the only options. What should you do?

3. Your grandfather is dying. While he is in this diminished state, you can easily persuade him to sign some legal documents that would give you sole rights to his large fortune upon his death. If he were fully coherent, he would never sign over his fortune to you. No one would ever learn of your deathbed swindle. Should you take the old man's money?

Endnote

1. Joel Feinberg, "Psychological Egoism," in *Moral Philosophy: Selected Readings,* ed. George Sher (San Diego: Harcourt Brace Jovanovich, 1987), 11–12.

CHAPTER 6

Utilitarianism

Are you a utilitarian? To find out, consider the following scenario: After years of research, a medical scientist—Dr. X—realizes that she is just one step away from developing a cure for all known forms of heart disease. Such a breakthrough would save hundreds of thousands of lives—perhaps millions. The world could finally be rid of heart attacks, strokes, heart failure, and the like, a feat as monumental as the eradication of deadly smallpox. That one last step in her research, however, is technologically feasible but morally problematic. It involves the killing of a single healthy human being to microscopically examine the person's heart tissue just seconds after the heart stops beating. The crucial piece of information needed to perfect the cure can be acquired only as just described; it cannot be extracted from the heart of a cadaver, an accident victim, someone suffering from a disease, or a person who has been dead for more than sixty seconds. Dr. X decides that the benefits to humanity from the cure are just too great to ignore. She locates a suitable candidate for the operation: a homeless man with no living relatives and no friends—someone who would not be missed. Through some elaborate subterfuge she manages to secretly do what needs to be done, killing the man and successfully performing the operation. She formulates the cure and saves countless lives. No one ever discovers how she obtained the last bit of information she needed to devise the cure, and she feels not the slightest guilt for her actions.

Did Dr. X do right? If you think so, then you may be a utilitarian. A utilitarian is more likely to believe that what Dr. X did was right, because it brought about consequences that were more good than bad. One man died, but countless others were saved.[1] In this example, we get a hint of some of the elements that have made utilitarianism so attractive (and often controversial) to so many. First, whether or not we agree with the utilitarian view in this case, we can see that it has some plausibility. We tend to think it entirely natural to judge the morality of an action by the effects that it has on the people involved. To decide if we do right or wrong, we want to know whether the consequences of our actions are good or bad, whether they bring pleasure or pain, whether they enhance or diminish the welfare of ourselves and others. Second, the utilitarian formula for distinguishing right and wrong actions seems exceptionally straightforward. We simply calculate which action among several possible actions has the best balance of good over evil, everyone considered, and act accordingly. Moral choice is apparently reduced to a single moral principle and simple math. Third, at least sometimes, we all seem to be utilitarians. We may tell a white lie because the truth would hurt someone's feelings. We may break a promise because keeping it causes more harm than good. We may want a criminal punished not because he broke the law but because the punishment may deter him from future crimes. We justify such departures from conventional morality on the grounds that they produce better consequences.

Utilitarianism is one of the most influential moral theories in history. The English philosopher Jeremy Bentham (1748–1832) was the first to fill out the theory in detail, and the English philosopher and economist John Stuart Mill (1806–1873) developed it further. In their hands, utilitarianism became a powerful instrument of social reform. It provided a rationale for promoting women's rights, improving the treatment of prisoners, advocating animal rights, and aiding the poor—all radical ideas in Bentham's and Mill's day. In the twenty-first century, the theory still has a strong effect on moral and policy decision making in many areas, including health care, criminal justice, and government.

Classic utilitarianism—the kind of act-utilitarianism formulated by Bentham—is the simplest form of the theory. It affirms the principle that the right action is the one that directly produces the best balance of happiness over unhappiness for all concerned. Happiness is an intrinsic good—the *only* intrinsic good. What matters most is how much net happiness comes directly from performing an action (as opposed to following a rule that applies to such actions). To determine the right action, we need only compute the amount of happiness that each possible action generates and choose the one that generates the most. There are no rules to take into account—just the single, simple utilitarian principle. Each set of circumstances calling for a moral choice is unique, requiring a new calculation of the varying consequences of possible actions.

Bentham called the utilitarian principle the **principle of utility** and asserted that all our actions can be judged by it. (Mill called it the **greatest happiness principle**.) As Bentham says,

> By the principle of utility is meant that principle which approves or disapproves of every action whatsoever, according to the tendency which it appears to have to augment or diminish the happiness of the party whose interest is in question: or, what is the same thing in other words, to promote or to oppose that happiness. . . .
>
> By utility is meant that property in any object, whereby it tends to produce benefit, advantage, pleasure, good, or happiness, (all this in the present case comes to the same thing) or (what comes again to the same thing) to prevent the happening of mischief, pain, evil, or unhappiness to the party whose interest is considered[.][2]

The principle of utility, of course, makes the theory consequentialist. The emphasis on happiness or pleasure makes it hedonistic, for happiness is the only intrinsic good.

As you can see, there is a world of difference between the moral focus of utilitarianism (in all its forms) and that of ethical egoism. The point of ethical egoism is to promote one's own good. An underlying tenet of utilitarianism is that you should promote the good of *everyone concerned* and that everyone *counts equally*. When deliberating about which action to perform, you must take into account your own happiness as well as that of everyone else who will be affected by your decision—and no one is to be given a privileged status. Such evenhandedness requires a large measure of impartiality, a quality that plays a role in every plausible moral theory. Mill says it best:

> [T]he happiness which forms the utilitarian standard of what is right in conduct, is not the agent's own happiness, but that of all concerned. As between his own happiness and that of others, utilitarianism requires him to be as strictly impartial as a disinterested and benevolent spectator.[3]

In classic act-utilitarianism, knowing how to tote up the amount of utility, or happiness, generated by various actions is essential. Bentham's answer to this requirement is the *hedonic calculus*, which quantifies happiness and handles the necessary calculations. His approach is straightforward in conception but complicated in the details: For each possible action in a particular situation, determine the total amount of happiness or unhappiness produced by it for one individual (that is, the *net* happiness—happiness minus unhappiness). Gauge the level of happiness with seven basic characteristics such as intensity, duration, and fecundity (how likely the pleasure or pain is to be followed by more pleasure or pain). Repeat this process for all individuals involved and sum their happiness or unhappiness to arrive at an overall net happiness for that particular action. Repeat for each possible action. The action with the best score (the most happiness or least unhappiness) is the morally right one.

Notice that in this arrangement, only the *total amount* of net happiness for each action matters. How the happiness is distributed among the persons involved does not figure into the calculations. This means that an action that affects ten people and produces 100 units of happiness is to be preferred over an action that affects those same ten people but generates only 50 units of happiness—even if most of the 100 units go to just one individual, and the 50 units divide equally among the ten. The aggregate of happiness is decisive; its distribution is not. Classic utilitarianism, though, does ask that any given amount of happiness be spread among as many people as possible—thus the utilitarian slogan "The greatest happiness for the greatest number."

Both Bentham and Mill define happiness as pleasure. In Mill's words,

> The creed which accepts as the foundation of morals *utility*, or the *greatest happiness principle*, holds that actions are right in proportion as they tend to promote happiness, wrong as they tend to produce the reverse of happiness. By "happiness" is intended

pleasure, and the absence of pain; by "unhappiness," pain, and the privation of pleasure.[4]

They differ, though, on the nature of happiness and how it should be measured. Bentham thinks that happiness varies only in quantity—different actions produce different amounts of happiness. To judge the intensity, duration, or fecundity of happiness is to calculate its quantity. Mill contends that happiness can vary in quantity *and* quality. There are lower pleasures, such as eating, drinking, and having sex, and there are higher pleasures, such as pursuing knowledge, appreciating beauty, and creating art. The higher pleasures are superior to the lower ones. The lower ones can be intense and enjoyable, but the higher ones are qualitatively better and more fulfilling. In this scheme, a person enjoying a mere taste of a higher pleasure may be closer to the moral ideal than a hedonistic glutton who gorges on lower pleasures. Thus Mill declared, "It is better to be a human being dissatisfied than a pig satisfied; better to be Socrates dissatisfied than a fool satisfied."[5] In Bentham's view, the glutton—who acquires a larger quantity of pleasure—would be closer to the ideal.

The problem for Mill is to justify his hierarchical ranking of the various pleasures. He tries to do so by appealing to what the majority prefers—that is, the majority of people who have experienced both the lower and higher pleasures. But this approach probably will not help, because people can differ drastically in how they rank pleasures. It is possible, for example, that a majority of people who have experienced a range of pleasures would actually disagree with Mill's rankings. In fact, any effort to devise such rankings using the principle of utility seems unlikely to succeed.

Many critics have argued that the idea of defining right action in terms of some intrinsic nonmoral good (whether pleasure, happiness, or anything else) is seriously problematic. Attempts to devise such a definition have been fraught with complications—a major one being that people have different ideas about what things are intrinsically valuable. Some utilitarians have tried to sidestep these difficulties by insisting that maximizing utility means maximizing people's *preferences*, whatever they are. This formulation seems to avoid some of the difficulties just mentioned but falls prey to another: some people's preferences may be clearly objectionable when judged by almost any moral standard, whether utilitarian or nonconsequentialist. Some people, after all, have ghastly preferences—preferences, say, for sexually abusing children or killing innocent people for fun. Some critics say that repairing this preference utilitarianism to avoid sanctioning objectionable actions seems unlikely without introducing some nonutilitarian moral principles such as justice, rights, and obligations.

Like act-utilitarianism, *rule-utilitarianism* aims at the greatest good for all affected individuals, but it maintains that we travel an indirect route to that goal. In rule-utilitarianism, the morally right action is not the one that directly brings about the greatest good but the one covered by a rule that, if followed consistently, produces the greatest good for all. In act-utilitarianism, we must examine each action to see how much good (or evil) it generates. Rule-utilitarianism would have us first determine what rule an action falls under, then see if that rule would likely maximize utility if everyone followed it. In effect, the rule-utilitarian asks, "What if everyone followed this rule?"

An act-utilitarian tries to judge the rightness of actions by the consequences they produce, occasionally relying on "rules of thumb" (such as "Usually we should not harm innocents") merely to save time. A rule-utilitarian, however, tries to follow every valid rule—even if doing so may not maximize utility in a specific situation.

In our example featuring Dr. X and the cure for heart disease, an act-utilitarian might compare the net happiness produced by performing the lethal operation and by not performing it, opting finally for the former because it maximizes happiness. A rule-utilitarian, on the other hand, would consider what moral rules seem to apply to the situation. One rule might be "It is permissible to conduct medical procedures or experiments on people without their full knowledge and consent in order to substantially advance medical science." Another one might say "Do not conduct medical procedures or experiments on people without their full knowledge and consent." If the first rule is generally followed, happiness is not likely to be maximized in the long run. Widespread adherence to this rule would encourage medical scientists and physicians to murder patients for the good of science. Such practices would outrage people and cause them to fear and distrust science and the medical profession, leading to the breakdown of the entire health care system and most medical research. But if the second rule is consistently adhered to, happiness is likely to be maximized over the long haul. Trust in physicians and medical scientists would be maintained, and promising research could continue as long as it was conducted with the patient's consent. The right action, then, is for Dr. X *not* to perform the gruesome operation.

APPLYING THE THEORY

Let us apply utilitarianism to another type of case. Imagine that for more than a year a terrorist has been carrying out devastating attacks in a developing country, killing hundreds of innocent men, women, and children. He seems unstoppable. He always manages to elude capture. In fact, because of his stealth, the expert assistance of a few accomplices, and his support among the general population, he will most likely never be captured or killed. The authorities have no idea where he hides or where he will strike next. But they are sure that he will go on killing indefinitely. They have tried every tactic they know to put an end to the slaughter, but it goes on and on. Finally, as a last resort, the chief of the nation's antiterrorist police orders the arrest of the terrorist's family—a wife and seven children. The chief intends to kill the wife and three of the children right away (to show that he is serious), then threaten to kill the remaining four unless the terrorist turns himself in. There is no doubt that the chief will make good on his intentions, and there is excellent reason to believe that the terrorist will indeed turn himself in rather than allow his remaining children to be executed.

Suppose that the chief has only two options: (1) refrain from murdering the terrorist's family and continue with the usual antiterrorist tactics (which have only a tiny chance of being successful) or (2) kill the wife and three of the children and threaten to kill the rest (a strategy with a very high chance of success). According to utilitarianism, which action is right?

As an act-utilitarian, the chief might reason like this: Action 2 would probably result in a net gain of happiness, everyone considered. Forcing the terrorist to turn himself in would save hundreds of lives. His killing spree would be over. The general level of fear and apprehension in the country might subside, and even the economy—which has slowed because of terrorism—might improve. The prestige of the terrorism chief and his agents might increase. On the downside, performing Action 2 would guarantee that four innocent people (and perhaps eight) would lose their lives, and the terrorist (whose welfare must also be included in the calculations) would be imprisoned for life or executed. In addition, many citizens would be disturbed by the killing of innocent people and the flouting of the law by the police, believing that these actions are wrong and likely to set a dangerous precedent. Over time, though, these misgivings may diminish. All things considered, then, Action 2 would probably produce more happiness than unhappiness. Action 1, on the other hand, maintains the status quo. It would allow the terrorist to continue murdering innocent people and spreading fear throughout the land—a decidedly unhappy result. It clearly would produce more unhappiness than happiness. Action 2, therefore, would produce the most happiness and would therefore be the morally right option.

As a rule-utilitarian, the chief might make a different choice. He would have to decide what rules would apply to the situation then determine which one, if consistently followed, would yield the most utility. Suppose he must decide between Rule 1 and Rule 2. Rule 1 says, "Do not kill innocent people in order to prevent terrorists from killing other innocent people." Rule 2 says, "Killing innocent people is permissible if it helps to stop terrorist attacks." The chief might deliberate as follows: We can be confident that consistently following Rule 2 would have some dire consequences for society. Innocent people would be subject to arbitrary execution, civil rights would be regularly violated, the rule of law would be severely compromised, and trust in government would be degraded. In fact, adhering to Rule 2 might make people more fearful and less secure than terrorist attacks would; it would undermine the very foundations of a free society. In a particular case, killing innocent people to fight terror could possibly have more utility than not killing them. But whether such a strategy would be advantageous to society over the long haul is not at all certain. Consistently following Rule 1 would have none of these unfortunate consequences. If so, a society living according to Rule 1 would be better off than one adhering to Rule 2, and therefore the innocent should not be killed to stop a terrorist.

EVALUATING THE THEORY

Bentham and Mill do not offer ironclad arguments demonstrating that utilitarianism is the best moral theory. Mill, however, does try to show that the principle of utility is at least a plausible basis for the theory. After all, he says, humans by nature desire happiness and nothing but happiness. If so, happiness is the standard by which we should judge human conduct, and therefore the principle of utility is the heart of morality. But this kind of moral argument is controversial because it reasons from what *is* to what *should be*. In addition, as pointed out in the discussion of psychological egoism, the notion that happiness is our sole motivation is dubious.

What can we learn about utilitarianism by applying the moral criteria of adequacy? Let us begin with classic act-utilitarianism and deal with rule-utilitarianism later. We can also postpone discussion of the minimum requirement of coherence, because critics have been more inclined to charge rule-utilitarianism than act-utilitarianism with having significant internal inconsistencies.

If we begin with Criterion 1 (consistency with considered judgments), we run into what some have called act-utilitarianism's most serious problem: it conflicts with commonsense views about justice. Justice requires equal treatment of persons. It demands, for example, that goods such as happiness be distributed fairly, and that we not harm one person to make several other persons happy. Utilitarianism says that everyone should be included in utility calculations, but it does not require that everyone get an equal share.

Consider this famous scenario from the philosopher H. J. McCloskey: While a utilitarian is visiting an area plagued by racial tension, a black man rapes a white woman. Race riots ensue, and white mobs roam the streets, beating and lynching black people as the police secretly condone the violence and do nothing to stop it. The utilitarian realizes that by giving false testimony, he could bring about the quick arrest and conviction of a black man whom he picks at random. As a result of this lie, the riots and the lynchings would stop, and innocent lives would be spared. As a utilitarian, he believes he has a duty to bear false witness to punish an innocent person.[6]

If right actions are those that maximize happiness, then it seems that the utilitarian would be doing right by framing the innocent person. The innocent person, of course, would experience unhappiness (he might be sent to prison or even executed), but framing him would halt the riots and prevent many other innocent people from being killed, resulting in a net gain in overall happiness. Framing the innocent is unjust, though, and our considered moral judgments would be at odds with such an action. Here the commonsense idea of justice and the principle of utility collide. The conflict raises doubts about act-utilitarianism as a moral theory.

Here is another famous example, by philosopher Judith Jarvis Thompson:

> This time you are to imagine yourself to be a surgeon, a truly great surgeon. Among other things you do, you transplant organs, and you are such a great surgeon that the organs you transplant always take. At the moment you have five patients who need organs. Two need one lung each, two need a kidney each, and the fifth needs a heart. If they do not get those organs today, they will all die; if you find organs for them today, you can transplant the organs and they will all live. But where to find the lungs, the kidneys, and the heart? The time is almost up when a report is brought to you that a young man who has just come into your clinic for his yearly check-up has exactly the right blood type, and is in excellent health. Lo, you have a possible donor. All you need do is cut him up and distribute his parts among the five who need them. You ask, but he says, "Sorry. I deeply sympathize, but no." Would it be morally permissible for you to operate anyway?[7]

This scenario involves the possible killing of an innocent person for the good of others. There seems little doubt that carrying out the murder and transplanting the victim's organs into five other people (and thus saving their lives) would maximize utility (assuming, of course, that the surgeon's deed would not become public, and that he or she suffered no untoward psychological effects, among other conditions). Compared to the happiness produced by doing the transplants, the unhappiness of the one unlucky donor seems minor. Therefore, according to act-utilitarianism, you (the surgeon) should commit the murder and do the transplants. But this choice appears to conflict with our considered moral judgments. Killing the healthy young man to benefit the five unhealthy ones seems unjust.

Consider one final case. Suppose a tsunami devastates a coastal town in Singapore. Relief agencies arrive on the scene to distribute food, shelter, and medical care to one hundred tsunami victims—disaster aid that amounts to, say, 1,000 units of happiness. There are only two options for the distribution of the 1,000 units. Option A is to divide the 1,000 units equally among all one hundred victims, supplying 10 units to each person. Option B is to give 901 units to one victim (who happens to be the richest person in town) and 99 units to the remaining victims, providing 1 unit per person. Both options distribute the same amount of happiness to the victims—1,000 units. Following the dictates of act-utilitarianism, we would have to say that the two actions (options) have equal utility and so are equally right. But this seems wrong. It seems unjust to distribute the units of happiness so unevenly when all recipients are equals in all morally relevant respects. Like the other examples, this one suggests that act-utilitarianism may be an inadequate theory.

Detractors also make parallel arguments against the theory in many cases besides those involving injustice. A familiar charge is that act-utilitarianism conflicts with our commonsense judgments both about people's rights and about their obligations to one another. Consider first this scenario about rights: Ms. Y is a nurse in a care facility for the elderly. She tends to many bedridden patients who are in pain most of the time, are financial and emotional burdens to their families, and are not expected to live more than a few weeks. Despite their misery, they do not wish for death; they want only to be free of pain. Ms. Y, an act-utilitarian, sees that there would be a lot more happiness in the world and less pain if these patients died sooner rather than later. She decides to take matters into her own hands, so she secretly gives them a drug that kills them quietly and painlessly. Their families and the facility staff feel enormous relief. No one will ever know what Ms. Y has done, and no one suspects foul play. She feels no guilt—only immense satisfaction knowing that she has helped make the world a better place.

If Ms. Y does indeed maximize happiness in this situation, then her action is right, according to act-utilitarianism. Yet most people would probably say that she violated the rights of her patients. The commonsense view is that people have certain rights that should not be violated merely to create a better balance of happiness over unhappiness.

Another typical criticism of act-utilitarianism is that it appears to fly in the face of our considered judgments about our obligations to other people. Suppose Mr. Z must decide between two actions: action A will produce 1,001 units of happiness; action B, 1,000 units. The only other significant difference between them is that action A entails the breaking of a promise. By act-utilitarian lights, Mr. Z should choose action A because it yields more happiness than action B does. But we tend to think that keeping a promise is more important than a tiny gain in happiness. We often try to keep our promises even when we know that doing so will result in a decrease in utility. Some say that if our obligations to others sometimes outweigh considerations of overall happiness, then act-utilitarianism must be problematic.[8]

What can an act-utilitarian say to rebut these charges about justice, rights, and obligations? One frequent response goes like this: The scenarios put forth by critics (such as the cases just cited) are misleading and implausible. They are always set up so that actions regarded as immoral produce the greatest happiness, leading to the conclusion that utilitarianism conflicts with commonsense morality and therefore cannot be an adequate moral theory. But in real life these kinds of actions almost never maximize happiness. In the case of Dr. X, her crime would almost certainly be discovered by physicians or other scientists, and she would be exposed as a murderer. This revelation would surely destroy her career, undermine patient-physician trust, tarnish the reputation of the scientific community, dry up funding for legitimate research, and prompt countless lawsuits. Scientists might even refuse to use the data from Dr. X's research because she obtained them through a heinous act. As one philosopher put it, "Given a clearheaded view of the world as it is and a realistic understanding of man's nature, it becomes more and more evident that injustice will never have, in the long run, greater utility than justice. . . . Thus injustice becomes, in actual practice, a source of great social disutility."[9]

The usual response to this defense is that the act-utilitarian is probably correct that most violations of commonsense morality do not maximize happiness—but at least some violations do. At least sometimes, actions that have the best consequences do conflict with our credible moral principles or considered moral judgments. The charge is that the act-utilitarian cannot plausibly dismiss all counterexamples, and only one counterexample is required to show that maximizing utility is not a necessary and sufficient condition for right action.[10]

Unlike ethical egoism, neither act-utilitarianism nor rule-utilitarianism fails Criterion 2 (consistency with our moral experiences), so we can move on to Criterion 3 (usefulness in moral problem solving). On this score, some scholars argue that act-utilitarianism deserves bad marks. Probably their most common complaint is what has been called the *no-rest problem*. Utilitarianism (in all its forms) requires that in our actions we *always* try to maximize utility, everyone considered. Say you are watching television. Utilitarianism would have you ask yourself, "Is this the best way to maximize happiness for everyone?" Probably not. You could be giving to charity or working as a volunteer for the local hospital or giving your coat to a homeless person or selling everything you own to buy food for hungry children. Whatever you are doing, there usually is something else you could do that would better maximize net happiness for everyone.

If act-utilitarianism does demand too much of us, then its usefulness as a guide to the moral life is suspect. One possible reply to this criticism is that the utilitarian burden can be lightened by devising rules that place limits on supererogatory actions (those generally considered above the call of duty). Another reply is that our moral common sense is simply wrong on this issue—we *should* be willing to perform, as our duty, many actions that are usually considered supererogatory. If necessary, we should be willing to give up our personal ambitions for the good of everyone. We should be willing, for example, to sacrifice a very large portion of our resources to help the poor.

To some, this reply seems questionable precisely because it challenges our commonsense moral intuitions—the very intuitions that we use to measure the plausibility of our moral judgments and principles. Moral common sense, they say, can be mistaken, and our intuitions can be tenuous or distorted—but we should cast them aside only for good reasons.

But a few utilitarians directly reject this appeal to common sense, declaring that relying so heavily on such intuitions is a mistake:

> Admittedly utilitarianism does have consequences which are incompatible with the common moral consciousness, but I tended to take the view "so much the worse for the common moral consciousness." That is, I was inclined to reject the common methodology of testing general ethical principles by seeing how they square with our feelings in particular instances.[11]

These utilitarians would ask, Isn't it possible that in dire circumstances, saving a hundred innocent lives by allowing one to die would be the best thing to do, even though allowing that one death would be a tragedy? Aren't there times when the norms of justice and duty *should* be ignored for the greater good of society?

To avoid the problems that act-utilitarianism is alleged to have, some utilitarians have turned to rule-utilitarianism. By positing rules that should be consistently followed, rule-utilitarianism seems to align its moral judgments closer to those of common sense. And the theory itself is based on ideas about morality that seem perfectly sensible:

> In general, rule utilitarianism seems to involve two rather plausible intuitions. In the first place, rule utilitarians want to emphasize that moral rules are important. Individual acts are justified by being shown to be in accordance with correct moral rules. In the second place, utility is important. Moral rules are shown to be correct by being shown to lead, somehow, to the maximization of utility. . . . Rule utilitarianism, in its various forms, tries to combine these intuitions into a single, coherent criterion of morality.[12]

But some philosophers have accused the theory of being internally inconsistent. They say, in other words, that it fails the minimum requirement of coherence. (If so, we can forgo discussion of our three criteria of adequacy.) They argue as follows: Rule-utilitarianism says that actions are right if they conform to rules devised to maximize utility. Rules with exceptions or qualifications, however, maximize utility better than rules without them. For example, a rule like "Do not steal except in these circumstances" maximizes utility better than the rule "Do not steal." It seems, then, that the best rules are those with amendments that make them as specific as possible to particular cases. But if the rules are changed in this way to maximize utility, they would end up mandating the same actions that act-utilitarianism does. They all would say, in effect, "Do not do this except to maximize utility." Rule-utilitarianism would lapse into act-utilitarianism.

Some rule-utilitarians respond to this criticism by denying that rules with a lot of exceptions would maximize utility. They say that people might fear that their own well-being would be threatened when others make multiple exceptions to rules. You might be reassured by a rule such as "Do not harm others" but feel uneasy about the rule "Do not harm others except in this situation." What if you end up in that particular situation?

Those who criticize the theory admit that it is indeed possible for an exception-laden rule to produce more unhappiness than happiness because of the anxiety it causes. But, they say, it is also possible for such a rule to generate a very large measure of happiness—large enough to more than offset any ill effects spawned by rule exceptions. If so, then rule-utilitarianism could easily slip into act-utilitarianism, thus exhibiting all of the conflicts with commonsense morality that act-utilitarianism is supposed to have.

LEARNING FROM UTILITARIANISM

Regardless of how much credence we give to the arguments for and against utilitarianism, we must admit that the theory seems to embody a large part of the truth about morality. First, utilitarianism begs us to consider that the consequences of our actions do indeed make a difference in our moral deliberations. Whatever factors work to make an action right (or wrong), surely the consequences of what we do must somehow be among them. Even if lying is morally wrong primarily because of the kind of act it is, we cannot plausibly think that a lie that saves a thousand lives is morally equivalent to one that changes nothing. Sometimes our considered moral judgments may tell us that an action is right regardless of the good (or evil) it does. And sometimes they may say that the good it does matters a great deal.

Second, utilitarianism—perhaps more than any other moral theory—incorporates the principle of impartiality, a fundamental pillar of morality itself. Everyone concerned counts equally in every moral decision. As Mill says, when we judge the rightness of our actions, utilitarianism requires us to be "as strictly impartial as a disinterested and benevolent spectator." Discrimination is forbidden, and equality reigns. We would expect no less from a plausible moral theory.

Third, utilitarianism is through and through a moral theory for promoting human welfare. At its core is the moral principle of beneficence—the obligation to act for the well-being of others. Beneficence is not the whole of morality, but to most people it is at least close to its heart.

KEYWORDS

greatest happiness principle—According to John Stuart Mill, the principle that "holds that actions are right in proportion as they tend to promote happiness, wrong as they tend to produce the reverse of happiness."

principle of utility—Jeremy Bentham's "principle which approves or dis-approves of every action whatsoever, according to the tendency which it appears to have to augment or diminish the happiness of the party whose interest is in question."

EXERCISES

Review Questions

1. Does utilitarianism incorporate the principle of impartiality? If so, how?
2. What is the main difference between the ways that Bentham and Mill conceive of happiness? Which view seems more plausible?
3. What is the difference between act-utilitarianism and rule-utilitarianism?
4. How do act-utilitarians and rule-utilitarians differ in their views on rules?
5. Is act-utilitarianism consistent with our considered moral judgments regarding justice? Why or why not?
6. To what was Mill referring when he said, "It is better to be a human being dissatisfied than a pig satisfied"?
7. How does Mill try to justify his hierarchical ranking of various pleasures?
8. Is the "no-rest problem" fatal for utilitarianism? Why or why not?
9. What would an act-utilitarian say about supererogatory acts?
10. What three truths about morality does utilitarianism seem to embody?

ETHICAL DILEMMAS

Explain how utilitarianism (act-utilitarianism or rule-utilitarianism) could be applied in the following scenarios to determine the proper course of action.

1. You are a doctor, and you have to decide which one of a dozen dying patients should receive a lifesaving drug, knowing that there is only enough of the medicine for one person. One of the patients is a skilled surgeon who has saved dozens of lives; the rest are homeless people, musicians, children, and ex-convicts. Which patient would you choose?
2. A married couple is trying to have a baby—specifically a male baby. In their society, females are undervalued and males are considered valuable assets for the family. Males are allowed to work in the facto-ries and to enter professions that are closed to females. The couple wants to ensure that they have only male children, so for years the wife has been going to the clinic to get sex-selection abortions—that

is, female fetuses are aborted but males are brought to term. Are these sex-selection abortions morally permissible?

3. A man is convicted of murder and is sentenced to life in prison. While serving his sentence, he has a change of heart and shows himself to be an excellent physician's assistant, successfully treating many prisoners in the infirmary and even saving lives. Prison officials know that the man is sincere, now completely harmless, and would probably save many lives if allowed to continue his work outside of prison. Suppose there are only two options: the man can serve out his life sentence, or he can be released from prison to work in a clinic serving poor people. Which is the right choice?

Endnotes

1. If you think that Dr. X did wrong, you may be a nonconsequentialist. A nonconsequentialist is likely to believe that Dr. X did wrong because of the nature of her action: it was murder. The consequences are beside the point.

2. Jeremy Bentham, "Of the Principle of Utility," in *An Introduction to the Principles of Morals and Legislation* (1789; reprint, Oxford: Clarendon Press, 1879), 1–7.

3. John Stuart Mill, "What Utilitarianism Is," in *Utilitarianism,* 7th ed. (London: Longmans, Green, 1879), Chapter II.

4. Mill, "What Utilitarianism Is," Chapter II.

5. Mill, "What Utilitarianism Is," Chapter II.

6. H. J. McCloskey, "A Non-Utilitarian Approach to Punishment," *Inquiry* 8 (1965): 239–49.

7. Judith Jarvis Thomson, "The Trolley Problem," in *Rights, Restitution, and Risk: Essays in Moral Theory,* ed. William Parent (Cambridge, MA: Harvard University Press, 1986), 95.

8. This case is based on one devised by W. D. Ross in *The Right and the Good* (Oxford: Clarendon Press, 1930), 34–35.

9. Paul W. Taylor, *Principles of Ethics: An Introduction* (Encino, CA: Dickenson, 1975), 77–78.

10. The points in this and the preceding paragraph were inspired by James Rachels, *The Elements of Moral Philosophy,* 4th ed. (Boston: McGraw-Hill, 2003), 111–12.

11. J. J. C. Smart, *Utilitarianism: For and Against* (Cambridge: Cambridge University Press, 1973), 68.

12. Fred Feldman, *Introductory Ethics* (Englewood Cliffs, NJ: Prentice-Hall, 1978), 77–78.

CHAPTER 7

Kantian Ethics

For the consequentialist, the rightness of an action depends entirely on the effects of that action (or on the effects of following the rule that governs the action). Good effects make the deed right; bad effects make the deed wrong. But for the nonconsequentialist (otherwise known as a **deontologist**), the rightness of an action can never be measured by such a variable, contingent standard as the quantity of goodness brought into the world. Rightness derives not from the consequences of an action but from its nature, its right-making characteristics. An action is right (or wrong) not because of what it produces but because of what it *is*. Yet for all their differences, both consequentialist and deontological theories contain elements that seem to go to the heart of morality and our moral experience. So in this chapter, we look at ethics through a deontological lens and explore Kant's moral system. We survey another major deontological view—natural law theory—in the next chapter.

The German philosopher Immanuel Kant (1724–1804) is considered one of the greatest moral philosophers of the modern era. Many scholars would go further and say that he is *the* greatest moral philosopher of the modern era. As a distinguished thinker of the Enlightenment, he sought to make reason the foundation of morality. For him, reason alone leads us to the right and the good. Therefore, to discover the true path we need not appeal to utility, religion, tradition, authority, happiness, desires, or intuition. We need only heed the dictates of reason, for reason informs us of the moral law just as surely as it reveals the truths of mathematics. Because of each person's capacity for reason, he or she is a sovereign in the moral realm, a supreme judge of what morality demands. What morality demands (in other words, our duty) is enshrined in the moral law—the changeless, necessary, universal body of moral rules.

In Kant's ethics, right actions have moral value only if they are done with a "good will"—that is, a will to do your duty for duty's sake. To act with a good will is to act with a desire to do your duty *simply because it is your duty*, to act out of pure reverence for the moral law. Without a good will, your actions have no moral worth—even if they accord with the moral law, even if they are done out of sympathy or love, even if they produce good results. Only a good will is unconditionally good, and only an accompanying good will can give your talents, virtues, and actions moral worth. As Kant explains,

> Nothing can possibly be conceived in the world, or even out of it, which can be called good without qualification, except a *good will*. Intelligence, wit, judgement, and the other *talents* of the mind, however they may be named, or courage, resolution, perseverance, as qualities of temperament, are undoubtedly good and desirable in many respects; but these gifts of nature may also become extremely bad and mischievous if the will which is to make use of them, and which, therefore, constitutes what is called *character*, is not good. It is the same with the *gifts of fortune*. Power, riches, honour, even health, and the general well-being and contentment with one's condition which is called *happiness*, inspire pride, and often presumption, if there is not a good will to correct the influence of these on the mind. . . . A good will is good not because of what it performs or effects, not by its aptness for the attainment of some proposed end, but simply by virtue of the volition—that is, it is good in itself, and considered by itself is to be esteemed much higher than all that can be brought about by it in favour of any inclination, nay, even of the sum-total of all inclinations.[1]

So to do right, we must do it for duty's sake, motivated solely by respect for the moral law. But how do we know what the moral law is? Kant sees the moral law as a set of principles, or rules, stated in the form of imperatives, or commands. Imperatives can be *hypothetical* or *categorical*. A **hypothetical imperative** tells us what we should do if we have certain desires: for example, "If you need money, work for it" or "If you want orange juice, ask for it." We should obey such imperatives only if we desire the outcomes specified. A **categorical imperative**, however, is not so iffy. It tells us that we should do something in all situations *regardless of our wants and needs*. A moral categorical imperative expresses a command like "Do not steal" or "Do not commit suicide." Such imperatives are universal and unconditional, containing no stipulations contingent on human desires or preferences. Kant says that the moral law consists entirely of categorical imperatives. They are the authoritative expression of our moral duties. Because they are the products of rational insight and we are rational agents, we can straightforwardly access, understand, and know them as the great truths that they are.

Kant says that all our duties, all the moral categorical imperatives, can be logically derived from a principle that he calls *the* categorical imperative. It tells us to "Act only on that maxim through which you can at the same time will that it should become a universal law."[2] (Kant actually devised three statements, or versions, of the principle: the one given here and two others; in the next few pages we will examine only the two most important ones.) Kant believed that every action implies a general rule, or maxim. If you steal a car, then your action implies a maxim such as "In this situation, steal a car if you want one." So the first version of the categorical imperative says that an action is right if you can will that the maxim of an action becomes a moral law applying to all persons. That is, an action is permissible if (1) its maxim can be universalized (if everyone can consistently act on the maxim in similar situations) and (2) you would be willing to let that happen. If you can so will the maxim, then the action is right (permissible). If you cannot, the action is wrong (prohibited). Right actions pass the test of the categorical imperative; wrong actions do not.

Some of the duties derived from the categorical imperative are, in Kant's words, perfect duties and some are imperfect duties. **Perfect duties** are those that absolutely must be followed without fail; they have no exceptions. Some perfect duties cited by Kant include duties not to break a promise, not to lie, and not to commit suicide. **Imperfect duties** are not always to be followed; they do have exceptions. As examples of imperfect duties, Kant mentions duties to develop your talents and to help others in need.

Kant demonstrates how to apply the first version of the categorical imperative to several cases, the most famous of which involves a lying promise. Imagine that you want to borrow money from someone, and you know you will not be able to repay the debt. You also know that you will get the loan if you falsely promise to pay the money back. Is such deceptive borrowing morally permissible? To find out, you have to devise a maxim for the action and ask whether you could consistently will it to become a universal law. Could you consistently will everyone to act on the maxim "If you need money, make a lying promise to borrow some"? Kant's emphatic answer is no. If all persons adopted this rule, then they would make lying promises to obtain loans. But then everyone would know that such promises are false, and the practice of giving loans based on a promise would no longer exist, because no promises could be trusted. If the maxim says that everyone should make a false promise in order to borrow money, then no one would loan money based on a promise. If acted on by everyone, the maxim would defeat itself. As Kant says, the "maxim would necessarily destroy itself as soon as it was made a universal law."[3] Therefore, you cannot consistently will the maxim to become a universal law. The action, then, is not morally permissible.

Kant believes that besides the rule forbidding the breaking of promises, the categorical imperative generates several other duties. Among these he includes prohibitions against committing suicide, lying, and killing innocent people.

Some universalized maxims may fail the test of the categorical imperative (first version) not by being self-defeating (as in the case of a lying promise) but by constituting rules that you would not want everyone else to act on. (Remember that an action is permissible if everyone can consistently act on it in similar situations *and* you would be willing to let that happen.) Kant asks us to consider a maxim that mandates *not* contributing anything to the welfare of others or aiding them when they are in distress. If you willed this maxim to become a universal moral law (if everyone followed it), no self-defeating state of affairs would result. Everyone could conceivably follow this rule. But you probably would not want people to act on this maxim because one day *you* may need *their* help and sympathy. Right now you may will the maxim to become universal law, but later, when the tables are turned, you may regret that policy. The inconsistency lies in wanting the rule to be universalized and not wanting it to be universalized. Kant says that this alternative kind of inconsistency shows that the action embodied in the maxim is not permissible.

Kant's second version of the categorical imperative is probably more famous and influential than the first. (Kant thought the two versions virtually synonymous, but they seem to be distinct principles.) He declares, "So act as to treat humanity, whether in thine own person or in that of any other, in every case as an end withal, never as means only."[4] This rule—the **means-ends principle**—says that we must always treat people (including ourselves) as ends in themselves, as creatures of great intrinsic worth, and never merely as things of instrumental value—that is, never merely as tools to be used for someone else's purpose.

This statement of the categorical imperative reflects Kant's view of the status of rational beings, or persons. Persons have intrinsic value and dignity because they, unlike the rest of creation, are rational agents who are free to choose their own ends, legislate their own moral laws, and assign value to things in the world. Persons are the givers of value, so they must have ultimate value. They therefore must always be treated as ultimate ends and never merely as means.

Kant's idea is that people not only have intrinsic worth, they also have *equal* intrinsic worth. Each rational being has the same inherent value as every other rational being. This equality of value cannot be altered by, and has no connection to, social and economic status, racial and ethnic considerations, or the possession of prestige or power. Any two persons are entitled to the same moral rights, even if one is rich, wise, powerful, and famous, and the other is not.

To treat people merely as a means rather than as an end is to fail to recognize the true nature and status of persons. Because people are by nature free, rational, autonomous, and equal, we treat them merely as a means if we do not respect these attributes—if we, for example, interfere with people's right to make informed choices by lying to them, inhibit their free and autonomous actions by enslaving or coercing them, or violate their equality by discriminating against them. For Kant, lying or breaking a promise is wrong because to do so is to use people merely as a means to an end, rather than as an end in themselves.

Sometimes we use people to achieve some end, yet our actions are not wrong. To see why, we must understand that there is a moral difference between treating persons as a means and treating them *merely*, or *only*, as a means. We may treat a mechanic as a means to repair our cars, but we do not treat him merely as a means if we also respect his status as a person. We do not treat him only as a means if we neither restrict his freedom nor ignore his rights.

As noted earlier, Kant insists that the two versions of the categorical imperative are two ways of stating the same idea. But the two principles seem to be distinct, occasionally leading to different conclusions about the rightness of an action. The maxim of an action, for example, may pass the first version and be permissible by being universalizable but fail the second by not treating persons as ends. A more plausible approach is to view the two versions not as alternative tests but as a single two-part test that an action must pass to be judged morally permissible. So before we can declare a maxim a bona fide categorical imperative, we must be able to consistently will it to become a universal law *and* know that it would have us treat persons not only as means but as ends.

APPLYING THE THEORY

How might a Kantian decide the case of the antiterrorist chief of police, discussed earlier, who considers killing a terrorist's wife and children? Recall that the terrorist is murdering hundreds of innocent people each year and that the chief has good reasons to believe that killing the wife and children (who are also innocent) will end the terrorist's attacks. Recall also the verdict on this case rendered from both the act-utilitarian and rule-utilitarian perspectives. By act-utilitarian lights, the chief should kill some of the terrorist's innocent relatives (and threaten to kill others). The rule-utilitarian view, however, is that the chief should *not* kill them.

Suppose the maxim in question is "When the usual antiterrorist tactics fail to stop terrorists from killing many innocent people, the authorities should kill (and threaten to kill) the terrorists' relatives." Can we consistently will this maxim to become a universal law? Does this maxim involve treating persons merely as a means to an end rather than an end in themselves? To answer the first question, we should try to imagine what would happen if everyone in the position of the relevant authorities followed this maxim. Would any inconsistencies or self-defeating states of affairs arise? We can see that the consequences of universalizing the maxim would not be pleasant. The authorities would kill the innocent—actions that could be as gruesome and frightening as terrorist attacks. But our willing that everyone act on the maxim would not be self-defeating or otherwise contradictory. Would we nevertheless be willing to live in a world where the maxim was universally followed? Again, there seems to be no good reason why we could not. The maxim therefore passes the first test of the categorical imperative.

To answer the second (means-ends) question, we must inquire whether following the maxim would involve treating someone merely as a means. The obvious answer is yes. This antiterrorism policy would use the innocent relatives of terrorists as a means to stop terrorist acts. Their freedom and their rights as persons would be violated. The maxim therefore fails the second test, and the acts sanctioned by the maxim would not be permissible. From the Kantian perspective, using the innocent relatives would be wrong no matter what—regardless of how many lives the policy would save or how much safer the world would be. So in this case, the Kantian verdict would coincide with that of rule-utilitarianism but not that of act-utilitarianism.

EVALUATING THE THEORY

Kant's moral theory meets the minimum requirement of coherence and is generally consistent with our moral experience (Criterion 2). In some troubling ways, however, it seems to conflict with our common-sense moral judgments (Criterion 1) and appears to have some flaws that restrict its usefulness in moral problem solving (Criterion 3).

As we saw earlier, some duties generated by the categorical imperative are absolute—they are, as Kant says, perfect duties, allowing no exceptions whatsoever. We have, for example, a perfect (exceptionless) duty not to lie—ever. But what should we do if lying is the only way to prevent a terrible tragedy? Suppose a friend of yours comes to your house in a panic and begs you to hide her from an insane man intent on murdering her. No sooner do you hide her in the cellar than the insane man appears at your door with a bloody knife in his hand and asks where your friend is. You have no doubt that the man is serious and that your friend will in fact be brutally murdered if the man finds her. Imagine that you have only two choices (and saying "I don't know" is not one of them): either you lie to the man and thereby save your friend's life, or you tell the man where she is hiding and guarantee her murder. Kant actually considers such a case and renders this verdict on it: you should tell the truth though the heavens fall. He says, as he must, that the consequences of your action here are irrelevant, and not lying is a perfect duty. There can be no exceptions. Yet Kant's answer seems contrary to our considered moral judgments. Moral common sense seems to suggest that in a case like this, saving a life would be much more important than telling the truth.

Another classic example involves promise keeping, which is also a perfect duty. Suppose you promise to meet a friend for lunch, and on your way to the restaurant you are called upon to help someone injured in a car crash. No one else can help her, and she will die unless you render aid. But if you help her, you will break your promise to meet your friend. What should you do? Kant would say that come what may, your duty is to keep your promise to meet your friend. Under these circumstances, however, keeping the promise just seems wrong.

These scenarios are significant because, contrary to Kant's view, we seem to have no absolute, or exceptionless, moral duties. We can easily imagine many cases like those just mentioned. Moreover, we can also envision situations in which we must choose between two allegedly perfect duties, each one prohibiting some action. We cannot fulfill both duties at once, and we must make a choice. Such conflicts provide plausible evidence against the notion that there are exceptionless moral rules.[5]

Conflicts of duties, of course, are not just deficiencies regarding Criterion 1. They also indicate difficulties with Criterion 3. Like many moral theories, Kant's system fails to provide an effective means for resolving major conflicts of duties.

Some additional inconsistencies with our common moral judgments seem to arise from applications of the first version of the categorical imperative. Remember that the first version says that an action is permissible if everyone can consistently act on it and if you would be willing to have that happen. At first glance, it seems to guarantee that moral rules are universally fair. But it makes the acceptability of a moral rule depend largely on whether *you personally* are willing to live in a world that conforms to the rule. If you are not willing to live in such a world, then the rule fails the first version of the categorical imperative, and your conforming to the rule is wrong. But if you are the sort of person who would prefer such a world, then conforming to the rule would be morally permissible. This subjectivity in Kant's theory could lead to the sanctioning of heinous acts of all kinds. Suppose the rule is "Kill everyone with dark skin" or "Murder all Jews." Neither rule would be contradictory if universalized; everyone could consistently act on it. Moreover, if you were willing to have everyone act on it—even willing to be killed if *you* have dark skin or are a Jew—then acts endorsed by the rule would be permissible. Thus the first version seems to bless acts that are clearly immoral.

Critics say that another difficulty with Kant's theory concerns the phrasing of the maxims to be universalized. Oddly enough, Kant does not provide any guidance for how we should state a rule describing an action, an oversight that allows us to word a rule in many different ways. Consider, for example, our duty not to lie. We might state the relevant rule like this: "Lie only to avoid injury or death to others." But we could also say "Lie only to avoid injury, death, or embarrassment to anyone who has green eyes and red hair (a group that includes you and your relatives)." Neither rule would lead to an inconsistency if everyone acted on it, so they both describe permissible actions. The second rule, though, is obviously not morally acceptable. More to the point, it shows that we could use the first version of the categorical imperative to sanction all sorts of immoral acts if we state the rule *in enough detail*. This result suggests not only a problem with Criterion 1 but also a limitation on the usefulness of the theory, a fault measured by Criterion 3. Judging the rightness of an action is close to impossible if the language of the relevant rule can change with the wind.

It may be feasible to remedy some of the shortcomings of the first version of the categorical imperative by combining it with the second. Rules such as "Kill everyone with dark skin" or "Lie only to avoid injury, death, or embarrassment to anyone who has green eyes and red hair" would be unacceptable because they would allow people to be treated merely as a means. But the means-ends principle itself appears to be in need of modification. The main difficulty is that our duties not to use people merely as a means can conflict, and Kant provides no counsel on how to resolve such dilemmas. Say, for example, that hundreds of innocent people are enslaved inside a brutal Nazi concentration camp, and the only way we can free them is to kill the Nazis guarding the camp. We must therefore choose between allowing the prisoners to be used merely as a means by the Nazis or using the Nazis merely as a means by killing them to free the prisoners.

Here is another example, a classic case from the philosopher C. D. Broad:

> Again, there seem to be cases in which you must either treat A or treat B, not as an end, but as a means. If we isolate a man who is a carrier of typhoid, we are treating him merely as a cause of infection to others. But, if we refuse to isolate him, we are treating other people merely as means to his comfort and culture.[6]

Kant's means-ends principle captures an important truth about the intrinsic value of persons. But we apparently cannot fully implement it, because sometimes we are forced to treat people merely as a means and not as ends in themselves.

LEARNING FROM KANT'S THEORY

Despite these criticisms, Kant's theory has been influential because it embodies a large part of the whole truth about morality. At a minimum, it promotes many of the duties and rights that our considered judgments lead us to embrace. In addition, it emphasizes three of morality's most important features: (1) universality, (2) impartiality, and (3) respect for persons.

Kant's first version of the categorical imperative rests firmly on universality—the notion that the moral law applies to all persons in relevantly similar situations. Impartiality requires that the moral law apply to everyone in the same way, that no one can claim a privileged moral status. In Kantian ethics, double standards are inherently bad. Ethical egoism fails as a moral theory in large part because it lacks this kind of impartiality. The first version of the categorical imperative, in contrast, enshrines impartiality as essential to the moral life. Kant's principle of respect for persons (the means-ends imperative) entails a recognition that persons have ultimate and inherent value, that they should not be used merely as a means to utilitarian ends, that equals should be treated equally, and that there are limits to what can be done to persons for the sake of good consequences. To many scholars, the central flaw of utilitarianism is that it does not incorporate a fully developed respect for persons. But in Kant's theory, the rights and duties of persons override any consequentialist calculus.

So Kantian ethics has many of the most important qualities that we associate with adequate moral theories. And no one has explained better than Kant why persons deserve full respect and how we are to determine whether persons are getting the respect they deserve.

KEYWORDS

categorical imperative—A command that we should follow regardless of our particular wants and needs; also, the single principle that defines Kant's ethical system, from which all additional maxims can be derived.

deontologist—One who believes that the rightness of an action derives not from the consequences of an action but from its nature (its right-making characteristics).

hypothetical imperative—A command that tells us what we should do if we have certain desires.

imperfect duty—A duty that has exceptions.

means-ends principle—The rule that we must always treat people (including ourselves) as ends in themselves, never merely as a means.

perfect duty—A duty that has no exceptions.

EXERCISES

Review Questions

1. What is the significance of a "good will" in Kant's ethics?
2. What is the difference between a hypothetical and a categorical imperative?
3. What is the moral principle laid out in the first version of Kant's categorical imperative?
4. What is the difference between perfect and imperfect duties?
5. How does Kant distinguish between treating someone as a means and treating someone *merely* as a means?
6. How can the absolutism of Kant's theory lead to judgments that conflict with moral common sense?
7. How might the subjectivity of Kant's theory lead to the sanctioning of heinous acts?
8. According to Kant, why is breaking a promise or lying immoral? Do you agree with Kant's reasoning?
9. In what way is Kant's ethics independent of (not based on) religious belief?
10. Give an example of how Kant's theory might conflict with our considered moral judgments.

ETHICAL DILEMMAS

Explain how Kant's theory could be applied in the following scenarios to determine the proper course of action.

1. Julie and Chan have been dating for three months, and their relationship has slowly blossomed into one of sincere affection and trust. At the time they began dating, Chan had a sexually transmitted disease, but he never disclosed this information to Julie. Without Julie's knowledge, Chan sought treatment and was eventually cured of the infection. Chan has kept his secret from the beginning and has no intention of ever revealing it to anyone. How would Kant evaluate this situation? Would he approve or disapprove of Chan's actions?

2. Imagine a World War II scenario in which German soldiers strap innocent people to the front of their tanks to dissuade Allied troops

from firing on the vehicles. If the Allies hold their fire, their positions will be overrun, and hundreds of their troops will be killed. The Allied commander, however, gives the order for his troops to shoot at the tanks anyway, knowing that the civilians will perish. Should the Allies kill these innocents?

3. In 1999, the dean of the Harvard Divinity School was fired from his university position because his office computer was found to contain pornography featuring sex between consenting adults. Otherwise the dean's behavior was exemplary, and his job performance was considered by Harvard to be of the highest caliber. Would Kant have also fired the dean, or would he have refused to do so on the grounds that firing him based on facts about his private life would be treating him merely as a means? Suppose Kant assumes that the dean's activities at the office were not part of his private life. What would Kant's verdict be then?

Endnotes

1. Immanuel Kant, *Fundamental Principles of the Metaphysic of Morals,* 2nd ed., trans. Thomas K. Abbott (London: Longmans, Green, 1879), 1–2.
2. Kant, *Fundamental Principles,* 52.
3. Kant, *Fundamental Principles,* 55.
4. Kant, *Fundamental Principles,* 66–67.
5. I owe this point to James Rachels, *The Elements of Moral Philosophy,* 4th ed. (Boston: McGraw-Hill, 2003), 126.
6. C. D. Broad, *Five Types of Ethical Theory* (1930; reprint, London: Routledge & Kegan Paul, 1956), 132.

CHAPTER 8

Natural Law Theory

The natural law theory of morality comes to us from ancient Greek and Roman philosophers (most notably, Aristotle and the Stoics) through the theologian and philosopher Thomas Aquinas (1225–1274). Aquinas molded it into its most influential form and bequeathed it to the world and the Roman Catholic Church, which embraced it as its official system of ethics. To this day, the theory is the primary basis for the Church's views on abortion, homosexuality, euthanasia, and other controversial issues.

Here we focus on the traditional version of the theory derived from Aquinas. This form is theistic, assuming a divine lawgiver who has given us the gift of reason to comprehend the order of nature. But there are other natural law theories of a more recent vintage that dispense with the religious elements, basing objective moral standards on human nature and the natural needs and interests of humans.

According to Aquinas, at the heart of the traditional theory is the notion that right actions are those that accord with the natural law—the moral principles that we can "read" clearly in the very structure of nature itself, including human nature. We can look into nature and somehow uncover moral standards because nature is a certain way: it is rationally ordered and teleological (goal-directed), with every part having its own purpose or end at which it naturally aims. From this notion about nature, traditional natural law theorists draw the following conclusion: how nature *is* reveals how it *should be*. The goals to which nature inclines reveal the values that we should embrace and the moral purposes to which we should aspire.

In conformity with an inherent, natural purpose or goal—that is, according to natural law—an acorn develops into a seedling, then into a sapling, and finally into an oak. The end toward which the acorn strives is the good (for acorns)—that is, to be a well-formed and well-functioning oak. Natural law determines how an oak functions—*and* indicates how an oak should function. If the oak does not function according to its natural purpose (if, for example, it is deformed or weak), it fails to be as it should be, deviating from its proper path laid down in natural law. Likewise, humans have a nature—a natural function and purpose unique among all living things. In human nature, in the mandates of the natural law for humanity, are the aims toward which human life strives. In these teleological strivings, in these facts about what human nature *is*, we can perceive what it *should be*.

What is it, exactly, that human nature aims at? Aquinas says that humans naturally incline toward preservation of human life, avoidance of harm, basic functions that humans and animals have in common (sexual intercourse, raising offspring, and the like), the search for truth, the nurturing of social ties, and behavior that is benign and reasonable. For humans, these inclinations constitute the good—the good of human flourishing and well-being. Our duty then is to achieve the good, to fully realize the goals to which our nature is already inclined. As Aquinas says,

> [T]his is the first precept of law, that *good is to be done and promoted, and evil is to be avoided.* All other precepts of the natural law are based upon this; so that all things which the practical reason naturally apprehends as man's good belong to the precepts of the natural law under the form of things to be done or avoided.
>
> Since, however, good has the nature of an end, and evil, the nature of the contrary, hence it is that all those things to which man has a natural inclination are naturally apprehended by reason as good, and consequently as objects of pursuit, and their contraries as evil, and objects of avoidance. Therefore, the order of the precepts of the natural law is according to the order of natural inclinations.[1]

In this passage, Aquinas refers to the aspect of human nature that enables us to decipher and implement the precepts of natural law: reason. Humans, unlike the rest of nature, are rational creatures, capable of understanding, deliberation, and free choice. Because all of nature is ordered and rational, only rational beings such as humans can peer into it and discern the inclinations in their nature, derive from the natural tendencies the natural laws, and apply the laws to their actions and their lives. Humans have the gift of reason (a gift from God, Aquinas says), and reason gives us access to the laws. Reason therefore is the foundation of morality. Judging the rightness of actions, then, is a matter of consulting reason, of considering rational grounds for moral beliefs.

It follows from these points that the natural (moral) laws are both objective and universal. The general principles of right and wrong do not vary from person to person or culture to culture. The dynamics of each situation may alter how a principle is applied, and not every situation has a relevant principle, but principles do not change with the tide. The natural laws are the natural laws. Further, they are not only binding on all persons, but they can be known by all persons. Aquinas insists that belief in God or inspiration from above is not a prerequisite for knowledge of morality. A person's effective use of reason is the only requirement.

Like Kant's categorical imperative, traditional natural law theory is, in the main, strongly absolutist. Natural law theorists commonly insist on several exceptionless rules. Directly killing the innocent is always wrong (which means that direct abortion is always wrong). Use of contraceptives is always wrong (on the grounds that it interferes with the natural human inclination toward procreation). Homosexuality is always wrong (again because it thwarts procreation). For Aquinas, lying, adultery, and blasphemy are always wrong.

As we have seen, moral principles—especially absolutist rules—can give rise to conflicts of duties. Kant's view on conflicting perfect duties is that such inconsistencies cannot happen. The natural law tradition gives a different answer: conflicts between duties are possible, but they can be resolved by applying the **doctrine of double effect.** This principle pertains to situations in which an action has both good and bad effects. It says that performing a good action may be permissible even if it has bad effects, but performing a bad action for the purpose of achieving good effects is never permissible. More formally, on a traditional interpretation of the doctrine, an action is permissible if four conditions are met:

1. *The action is inherently (without reference to consequences) either morally good or morally neutral.* That is, the action itself must at least be morally permissible.

2. *The bad effect is not used to produce the good effect (though the bad may be a side effect of the good).* Killing a fetus to save the mother's life is never permissible. However, using a drug to cure the mother's life-threatening disease—even though the fetus dies as a side effect of the treatment—may be permissible.

3. *The intention must always be to bring about the good effect.* For any given action, the bad effect may occur, and it may even be foreseen, but it must not be intended.

4. *The good effect must be at least as important as the bad effect.* The good of an action must be proportional to the bad. If the bad heavily outweighs the good, the action is not permissible. The good of saving your own life in an act of self-defense, for example, must be at least as great as the bad of taking the life of your attacker.

The doctrine of double effect is surprisingly versatile. Natural law theorists have used it to navigate moral dilemmas in medical ethics, reproductive health, warfare, and other life-and-death issues. The next section provides a demonstration.

APPLYING THE THEORY

Traditional natural law theory and its double-effect doctrine figure prominently in obstetrics cases in which a choice must be made between harming a pregnant woman or her fetus. A typical scenario goes something like this: A pregnant woman has cancer and will die unless she receives chemotherapy to destroy the tumors. If she does take the chemotherapy, the fetus will die. Is it morally permissible for her to do so?

In itself, the act of taking the chemotherapy is morally permissible. There is nothing inherently wrong with using a medical treatment to try to cure a life-threatening illness. So the action meets Condition 1. We can also see that the bad effect (killing the fetus) is not used to produce the good effect (saving the woman's life). Receiving the chemotherapy is the method used to achieve the good effect. The loss of the fetus is an indirect, unintended result of the attempt to destroy the cancer. The action therefore meets Condition 2. The intention behind the action is to kill the cancer and thereby save the woman's life—not to kill the fetus. The woman and her doctors know that the unfortunate consequence of treating the cancer will be the death of the fetus. They foresee the death, but their intention is not to kill the fetus. Thus, the action meets Condition 3. Is the good effect proportional to the bad effect? In this case, a life is balanced against a life, the life of the woman and the life of the fetus. From the natural law perspective, both sides of the scale seem about equal in importance. If the good effect to be achieved for the woman was, say, a nicer appearance through cosmetic surgery, and the bad effect was the death of the fetus, the two sides would not have the same level of importance. But in this case, the action does meet Condition 4. Because the action meets all four conditions, receiving the chemotherapy is morally permissible for the woman.

Now let us examine a different kind of scenario. Remember that we earlier applied both utilitarianism and Kant's theory to the anti-terrorism tactic of killing a terrorist's relatives. To stop the murder of many innocent people by a relentless terrorist, the authorities consider killing his wife and three of his children and threatening to kill the remaining four children. What verdict would the doctrine of double effect yield in this case?

Here the action is the antiterrorist tactic just described. The good effect is preventing the death of innocent citizens; the bad effect is the killing of other innocents. Right away we can see that the action, in itself, is not morally good. Directly killing the innocent is never permissible, so the action does not meet Condition 1. Failing to measure up to even one condition shows the action to be prohibited, but we will continue our analysis anyway. Is the bad effect used to produce the good effect? Yes. The point of the action is to prevent further terrorist killings, and the means to that end is killing the terrorist's wife and children. The bad is used to achieve the good. So the action does not meet Condition 2, either. It does, however, meet Condition 3 because the intention behind the action is to bring about the good effect, preventing further terrorist killings. Finally, if we view the good effect (preventing the deaths of citizens) as comparable to the bad effect (the killing of the terrorist's wife and children), we should infer that the action meets Condition 4. In any case, because the action fails Conditions 1 and 2, we have to say that the action of the authorities (killing members of the terrorist's family) is not permissible.

As suggested earlier, a Kantian theorist would likely agree with this decision, and a rule-utilitarian would probably concur. However, judging that the good consequences outweigh the bad, an act-utilitarian might very well say that killing the wife and children to prevent many other deaths would not only be permissible but obligatory.

EVALUATING THE THEORY

Traditional natural law theory appears to contain no crippling internal inconsistencies, so we will regard it as an eligible theory for evaluation. But it does encounter difficulties with Criteria 1 and 3.

The theory seems to fall short of Criterion 1 (conflicts with common-sense moral judgments) in part because of its absolutism, a feature that also encumbers Kant's theory. As we have seen, natural law theorists maintain that some actions are *always* wrong: for example, intentionally killing the innocent, impeding procreation (through contraception, sterilization, or sexual preferences), or lying. Such absolutes, though, can lead to moral judgments that seem to diverge from common sense. The absolute prohibition against directly killing the innocent, for example, could actually result in great loss of life in certain extreme circumstances. Imagine that a thousand innocent people are taken hostage by a homicidal madman, and the only way to save the lives of 999 of them is to intentionally kill one of them. If the one is not killed, all one thousand will die. Most of us would probably regard the killing of the one hostage as a tragic but necessary measure to prevent a massive loss of life. The alternative—letting them all die—would seem a much greater tragedy. But many natural law theorists would condemn the killing of the one innocent person even if it would save the lives of hundreds.

Similarly, suppose a pregnant woman will die unless her fetus is aborted. Would it be morally permissible for her to have the abortion? Given the natural law prohibition against killing the innocent, many natural law theorists would say no. Aborting the fetus would be wrong even to save the mother's life. But most people would probably say that this view contradicts our considered moral judgments.

The absolutism of natural law theory arises from the notion that nature is authoritatively teleological. Nature aims toward particular ends that are ordained by the divine, and the values inherent in this arrangement cannot and must not be ignored or altered. How nature *is* reveals how it *should be*. Period. But the teleological character of nature has never been established by logical argument or empirical science—at least not to the satisfaction of most philosophers and scientists. In fact, science (including evolutionary theory) suggests that nature is not teleological at all but instead random and purposeless, changing and adapting according to scientific laws, blind cause and effect, chance mutation, and competition among species. Moreover, the idea that values can somehow be extracted from the facts of nature is as problematic for natural law theory as it is for ethical egoism and utilitarianism. From the fact that humans have a natural inclination toward procreation it does not follow that discouraging procreation through contraception is morally wrong.

Natural law theory seems to falter on Criterion 3 (usefulness) because, as just mentioned, discovering what values are inscribed in nature is problematic. The kind of moral principles that we might extract from nature depends on our conception of nature, and such conceptions can vary. Taking their cue from Aquinas, many natural law theorists see the inclinations of human nature as benign; others, as fundamentally depraved. Historically, humans have shown a capacity for both great good and monstrous evil. Which inclination is the true one? And even if we could accurately identify human inclinations, there seems to be no reliable procedure for uncovering the corresponding moral values or telling whether moral principles should be absolutist.

LEARNING FROM NATURAL LAW

Like Kantian ethics, natural law theory is universalist, objective, and rational, applying to all persons and requiring that moral choices be backed by good reasons. The emphasis on reason makes morality independent of religion and belief in God, a distinction also found in Kant's ethics. At the heart of natural law theory is a strong respect for human life, an attitude that is close to, but not quite the same thing as, Kant's means-ends principle. Respect for life or persons is, of course, a primary concern of our moral experience and seems to preclude the kind of wholesale ends-justify-the-means calculations that are a defining characteristic of many forms of utilitarianism.

Natural law theory emphasizes a significant element in moral deliberation that some other theories play down: intention. In general, intention plays a larger role in natural law theory than it does in Kant's categorical imperative. To many natural law theorists, the rightness of an action often depends on the intentions of the moral agent performing it. In our previous example of the pregnant woman with cancer, for example, the intention behind the act of taking the chemotherapy is to kill the cancer, not the fetus, though the fetus dies because of the treatment. So the action is thought to be morally permissible. If the intention had been to directly kill the fetus, the action would have been deemed wrong. In our everyday moral experience, we frequently take intentions into account in evaluating an action. We usually would think that there must be some morally relevant difference between a terrorist's intentionally killing ten people and a police officer's accidentally killing those same ten people while chasing the terrorist, though both scenarios result in the same tragic loss of life.

KEYWORD

doctrine of double effect—The principle that performing a good action may be permissible even if it has bad effects, but performing a bad action for the purpose of achieving good effects is never permissible; any bad effects must be unintended.

EXERCISES

Review Questions

1. In what way is natural law theory rational?
2. According to natural law theorists, how can nature reveal anything about morality?
3. According to Aquinas, what is the good that human nature aims at?
4. According to natural law theory, how are moral principles objective? How are they universal?
5. Explain what the following statement means: "How nature *is* reveals how it *should be*."
6. What is the main criticism of the absolutism of traditional natural law theory?
7. What part do intentions play in the doctrine of double effect?
8. What is the first condition of the doctrine of double effect?
9. What does it mean to say that nature is authoritatively teleological?
10. In natural law theory, how are the moral rules supposed to be discerned—through intuition, reason, or utilitarian principles?

ETHICAL DILEMMAS

Explain how natural law theory could be applied in the following scenarios to determine the proper course of action.

1. A scientist is conducting an experiment using one hundred adult subjects, hoping to finally discover a cure for liver cancer. Conducting this one last study is the only way to identify the substance that can cure the disease and save the lives of countless people. But the experiment causes long-lasting, horrible pain in the subjects, and they will not be able to benefit in any way from the study's success. The researcher would ordinarily never be able to enlist any subjects for the study because of these two facts, so to ensure the cooperation of the subjects, he lies to them: he says that being a part of the study will be painless and that it will increase their life span. The study is completed, the cure is found, and the subjects spend the next year in agony. What would natural law theory say about the scientist's actions?

2. Thirty people are trapped in a cave that will soon fill with ocean water and drown them. The only way out is an opening in the cave wall, but it is blocked by an obese man who is wedged firmly in the breach— and no amount of pulling or pushing can dislodge him. The leader of the group, however, has several sticks of dynamite that could be used to blast a hole in the opening, freeing everyone but killing the obese man. Should the man be sacrificed to save everyone? Should the others spare him and thus bring death to them all?

3. A pregnant woman has undergone prenatal testing and now knows that the fetus she is carrying has Down syndrome, a congenital disease characterized by moderate to severe mental retardation and facial disfigurement. The woman has been given a choice: abort the fetus and avoid having a Down syndrome baby, or carry the baby to term and hope that the effects of the disease are not too severe. What would natural law theory have her do?

Endnote

1. Thomas Aquinas, *Summa Theologica*, in *Basic Writings of Saint Thomas Aquinas,* ed. and annotated by Anton C. Pegis (New York: Random House, 1945), First Part of the Second Part, Question 94, Article 2.

CHAPTER 9

Social Contract Theory

So far we have examined several moral theories and observed that each is based on, and justified by, some distinctive fundamental feature. For utilitarianism, the feature is utility; for the divine command theory, God's will; for Kant, the categorical imperative; for natural law theory, teleological nature. But suppose you don't believe in any of these justifying principles. You think the universe is entirely physical—just atoms in motion, devoid of divinity and purpose. You believe reason can never yield an authoritative rational principle like the categorical imperative, and you are sure that utilitarianism is hopelessly unrealistic because people can never be trusted to promote the common good. At their core, people are egoistic and self-interested. And in service to their own needs and desires, they will, given the chance, commit all manner of horrific cruelties and vile wrongs. In such a world, on what foundation can morality rest? In such a perilous and corrosive environment, how can morality ever find a foothold?

For some, the answer is **social contract theory** (or *contractarianism*). This doctrine says morality arises from a social contract that self-interested and rational people would abide by in order to secure a degree of peace, prosperity, and safety. Without such an agreement, life would be nearly unlivable, with each person competing with everyone else to promote his or her own interests, to grab as much wealth and power as possible, and to defend his or her person and property against all comers. Humanity, as the saying goes, would be red in tooth and claw. But such a dog-eat-dog world is in no one's interests. Only in a world where people restrain their greed and try to cooperate with one another can they achieve a modestly satisfying and secure life. And this kind of restraint and cooperation, says the social contract theorist, is possible only through a social contract in which people agree to obey practical, beneficial rules as long as everyone else does the same. Obedience means relinquishing some personal freedom and giving up the option to kill, wound, and cheat our neighbors at will, but it also ensures a better life and a measure of protection from the ravages of continual conflict and fear. From this social contract comes morality, for the rules *constitute* morality. Morality comprises the social rules that are in everyone's best interests to heed. In a well-ordered society, the rules are embodied in laws and policies, enforced by the state and recognized by most citizens as necessary and legitimate. They are deemed legitimate because they are the result of an agreement among rational equals who understand that the contract, however restrictive, is for the best.

HOBBES'S THEORY

The first well-developed social contract theory in modern times was devised by the British philosopher and linguist Thomas Hobbes (1588–1679). He argues for the necessity of a social contract by first giving us a glimpse of a world without one. In his masterpiece *Leviathan*, he presents a pessimistic picture of human beings in their natural, unfettered, lawless state. They are, he says, greedy, selfish, violent, self-destructive, and desperate. Their cutthroat struggle for advantage and survival rages on and on because they are roughly equal in strength and ability, ensuring that no one can win. So conflict, chaos, death, and loss reign—and humankind is reduced to living in a horrifying and gruesome "state of nature." This state is not merely a Hobbesian construct: it arises in the real world when there is a breakdown in the forces that preserve law and order—in times of revolution, war, natural disaster, famine, and civil unrest. According to Hobbes,

> Hereby it is manifest, that during the time men live without a common power to keep them all in awe, they are in that condition which is called war; and such a war, as is of every man, against every man. . . .

Whatsoever therefore is consequent to a time of war, where every man is enemy to every man; the same is consequent to the time; wherein men live without other security, than what their own strength, and their own invention shall furnish them withal. In such condition, there is no place for industry; because the fruit thereof is uncertain: and consequently no culture of the earth; no navigation, nor use of the commodities that may be imported by sea; no commodious building; no instruments of moving, and removing such things as require much force; no knowledge of the face of the earth; no account of time; no arts; no letters; no society; and which is worst of all, continual fear, and danger of violent death; and the life of man, solitary, poor, nasty, brutish, and short.[1]

As long as people continue to trample others on the way to steal the biggest piece of pie, life will remain a "war of every man against every man." The only rational alternative, says Hobbes, is to accept a social contract that mandates cooperation and restraint. By following the rules, everyone wins. The agreement will prohibit contract breaking as well as harming, threatening, and defrauding others, because such behavior threatens the peace and prosperity that the social contract makes possible.

But people are people, and they will renege on the deal if given half a chance. So Hobbes says what's needed is a fearsome, powerful person or persons to enforce the rules, to threaten punishment, and to deliver it swiftly to rule breakers. Specifically, what's required is an absolute sovereign, what Hobbes refers to as the Leviathan (the name of a terrifying monster mentioned in the Bible). The Leviathan's job is to ensure that the social contract is honored and that agreements are kept. His subjects agree to cede to him much of their freedom and right of self-determination in exchange for an orderly and secure society.

Before the Leviathan rules society, Hobbes says, there is no right and wrong:

[In the state of nature] nothing can be unjust. The notions of right and wrong, justice and injustice have there no place. . . . It is consequent also to the same condition, that there be no propriety, no dominion, no mine and thine distinct; but only that to be every man's, that he can get; and for so long, as he can keep it.[2]

Morality comes into existence only when the Leviathan takes control and guarantees the strength and stability of the social contract.

PLUSES AND MINUSES

Many thinkers have tried to improve on Hobbes's theory or offer alternatives, and the result is that several types of social contract theory have been put forth. But let's limit our discussion to Hobbes's system (and those like it). As with every major moral system, Hobbesian social contract theory has both appealing and questionable features, so let's examine both.

On the positive side, the theory provides an answer to skeptics and relativists who question whether morality is objective or consists of a set of beliefs we merely happen to accept. It says that morality is objective because it consists of the rules—the standards of right and wrong—that rational members of society have determined to be most beneficial for all. The source of morality is therefore apparent. We need not ask—as we would with many other theories—whether it is based on God's will, teleological nature, or pure reason. They make peaceful coexistence and productive cooperation possible, and they are the very rules that would be enacted by rational people of equal status whose goal is to see that the rules benefit everyone.

These attributes ensure that, at least in one respect, Hobbes's theory scores high on the moral criterion of usefulness: there is no mystery about how to find out if an action is morally right or wrong. The social rules are those that promote social harmony. It is clear that theft, murder, fraud, promise breaking, exploitation, intolerance, and other malicious acts are contrary to social order, so they are immoral.

But why should we be moral in the first place? Or to put it another way, What is the purpose of morality? This is a difficult question for any moral theory. The social contract answer is straightforward: We should be moral in a society where the rules are generally followed because we are better off doing so. In addition, breaking the rules would bring punishment from the Leviathan, and trying to avoid the pain of such punishment is rational.

Philosophers have faulted Hobbes's theory on several counts. Among the most important of these is the charge that few people have ever actually *consented* to the terms of a social contract. (Critics make this point against other forms of the theory, not just Hobbes's.) The essence of a contract is that people freely agree to abide by its terms. Presumably, if they don't give their consent, they are not obliged to obey the contract's rules. But who has explicitly agreed to be bound by a social contract? Who has raised their right hand and sworn allegiance or signed on the dotted line? Most people have not.

Some defenders of social contract theory reply that people may not have given their explicit consent, but they surely have given their *implicit* consent. By enjoying the social and material advantages that the social contract makes possible, these advocates say, people implicitly agree to abide by its rules. If they accept the benefits, they tacitly agree to shoulder the obligations.

But this notion of implicit consent will not do. There are many who benefit from living in a well-ordered society, but we cannot plausibly say they consented to be bound by any social contract. People are born into a particular society without their consent; they have no choice in the matter. They do not agree to be part of the social order. And as adults, many may hate the society they find themselves in but cannot leave it because the political, financial, and social costs of trying to emigrate may be prohibitive. In any case, it is hard to see how such citizens could be said to implicitly accept a social contract.

At this point the contractarian might say that we can be duty-bound to obey the moral tenets of a social contract even if we *don't* consent to it, either explicitly or implicitly. Our moral duties are established not because we accept the social contract from which they come, but because the contract is one that we *would* embrace if we were rational individuals searching for rules that would best serve everyone's interests. The social contract, in other words, is hypothetical but nevertheless binding. This is how most contemporary contractarians view social contracts. They see them as fictions—but very useful fictions. For example, today's most influential social contract theory comes from the philosopher John Rawls (1921–2002). He attempted to determine what moral principles a society would accept if they were arrived at through a hypothetical give-and-take that was as fair and impartial as possible. According to Rawls, such principles are what "free and rational persons concerned to further their own interests would accept in an initial position of equality as defining the fundamental terms of their association."[3]

There is a stronger objection that has been made against Hobbes's theory and contractarian theories generally: the category of individuals that we normally think should have moral status is restricted. Living beings have moral status if they are suitable candidates for moral concern or respect. This means we cannot treat them just any way we want; we have direct moral duties to them. We know that normal, rational, adult human beings have full moral status—they deserve our highest level of respect and consideration no matter their social situation. And we typically think that vulnerable individuals—for example, the severely disabled, the very poor, nonhuman animals, children, and infants—also have moral status: they also deserve a measure of our respect and consideration. But critics charge that social contract theories conflict with these intuitions. The theories generally hold that the only ones who have moral status are those who can legitimately be party to a social contract (the contractors), and the only ones who can participate in a social contract are those for whom participation would be mutually beneficial. The vulnerable individuals who cannot take part in this give-and-take for mutual benefit may have no moral status and no rights.

Modern contractarians have responded to these complaints in several ways. Their general contention is that although vulnerable individuals may not be contractors, it does not follow that they can be mistreated or left unprotected. They point out, for example, that it may be mutually advantageous for society to care for disabled children because some contractors (namely, parents) care about such children, and this concern makes the benevolent treatment of disabled children a matter of the parents' self-interest. Also, it may be in everyone's interests for society to care for the elderly, the chronically ill, and victims of accidents, because in the future we all may find ourselves in one of these situations. Or benefiting the vulnerable could be viewed as a psychological need of contractors, so fulfilling this need by helping the vulnerable may be in every contractor's best interests.

KEYWORD

social contract theory—The doctrine that morality arises from a social contract that self-interested and rational people would abide by in order to secure a degree of peace, prosperity, and safety.

EXERCISES

Review Questions

1. According to Hobbes, where does morality come from?
2. On what view of human behavior is Hobbes's social contract theory based?
3. Why does Hobbes insist that a Leviathan is a necessary part of the social contract?

4. According to Hobbes, what usually happens when there is no common power to keep people in line?
5. According to Hobbes, when does morality arise in a society?
6. What are the main features of the state of nature, according to Hobbes?
7. When, according to Hobbes, does injustice come into being?
8. Does Hobbes think there is an equality of ability among people, or does he believe that the strength and abilities of humans vary tremendously?
9. According to Hobbes, when does society become a "war of every man against every man"?
10. What form of government does Hobbes prefer—democracy, meritocracy, or dictatorship?

ETHICAL DILEMMAS

Explain how social contract theory could be applied in the following scenarios to determine the proper course of action.

1. Your country is in the middle of a revolution and lawlessness prevails. You know that some of your neighbors are starving, but you have plenty of food for everyone. Are you obligated to give some of that food to them? Why or why not?
2. A ruthless Leviathan has assumed power in your nation, and he has issued many stern rules to ensure peace and prosperity. The punishment for breaking one of these rules is long imprisonment or death. Unfortunately, you may have to break a rule against lying to public officials, because telling the truth would condemn a friend of yours to lifelong imprisonment for a crime you know he did not commit. Should you lie?
3. The Leviathan who rules the kingdom has been enforcing the laws of the land with an iron fist. Minor infractions like double parking are usually punished with beatings so severe that some people have died from their injuries. Because of such incidents, many citizens say the Leviathan acts unjustly, and they launch a revolution to overthrow the despot. Should you join the revolution or respect the laws? Why or why not?

Endnotes

1. Thomas Hobbes, *Leviathan*, 1651.
2. Hobbes, *Leviathan*.
3. John Rawls, *A Theory of Justice*, rev. ed. (Cambridge, MA: Harvard University Press, 1999), 10.

CHAPTER 10

The Feminist Challenge

Beyond the moral theorizing of Aquinas, Kant, Hobbes, and Mill, there is a different approach to moral thinking and feeling that constitutes a serious challenge to them: **feminist ethics**. Feminist ethics is not a moral theory so much as an alternative way of looking at the concepts and concerns of the moral life. It is an approach focused on women's interests and experiences and devoted to supporting the moral equality of women and men.

Those who see ethics from this perspective are reacting to some hard facts. One is that most of the great ethical theorists (and many of their followers, past and present) have assumed that women are somehow morally inferior to men—less rational, less important, less mature, or less moral. Coupled with this bias is a trend that is even more alarming: most women throughout the world are in a thousand ways second-class citizens (or worse). By law, by religion, or by custom, they are the victims of violence, stereotype, bigotry, coercion, forced dependence, and social, political, and professional inequality. Modern Western societies are as guilty of some of these evils as many countries in the developing world.

In the West, some ways of thinking and feeling have been regarded as characteristic of women, and these ways, whether distinctive of women or not, have been largely neglected by moral philosophers (who have traditionally been men). According to the feminist philosopher Alison M. Jaggar,

> Western moral theory is said to embody values that are "masculine," insofar as they are associated, empirically, normatively, or symboli-

cally, with men. For instance, western ethics is alleged to prefer the supposedly masculine or male-associated values of independence, autonomy, intellect, will, wariness, hierarchy, domination, culture, transcendence, product, asceticism, war and death over the supposedly feminine or female-associated values of interdependence, community, connection, sharing, emotion, body, trust, absence of hierarchy, nature, immanence, process, joy, peace and life.[1]

Some moral issues are more likely to arise from women's experiences than men's, and these too have been overlooked:

> Issues of special concern to women are said to have been ignored by modern moral philosophers, who have tended to portray the domestic realm as an arena outside the economy and beyond justice, private in the sense of being beyond the scope of legitimate political regulation. Even philosophers like Aristotle or Hegel (1770–1831), who give some ethical importance to the domestic realm, have tended to portray the home as an arena in which the most fully human excellences are incapable of being realized. . . . [Feminist philosophers] argued that the philosophical devaluation of the domestic realm made it impossible to raise questions about the justice of the domestic division of labor, because it obscured the far-reaching social significance and creativity of women's work in the home, and concealed, even legitimated, the domestic abuse of women and girls.[2]

In the past few decades, feminist philosophers and other thinkers (mostly women but some men) have tried to shed light on all of these dark corners. The result—still an ongoing project—is feminist ethics and its grandchild, the ethics of care.

FEMINIST ETHICS

Feminists are a diverse group with contrasting viewpoints, so it should not be a surprise that they approach feminist ethics in different ways and arrive at different conclusions. Still, some generalizations are possible.

An emphasis on personal relationships. For the most part, traditional moral theories have been concerned with what we could call "public life"—the realm where unrelated individuals try to figure out how to behave toward one another and how to ensure that, among strangers, justice is done, rights are respected, and utility is maximized. The focus has been mostly on moral judgments and theories pertaining to people as separate members of the community, the polity, and the culture. But feminist ethics narrows the area of moral concern down to the interconnected and familiar small group—to the people with whom we have close personal relationships. The relationships of interest are the ties of kinship, the bonds of friendship, or the connections between caregivers and the cared-for—the sphere of the domestic and the private. This is the realm of intimate relations, sexual behavior, child rearing, and family struggles—the place we all come from and perhaps never leave, and where we live a large part of our moral lives.

A suspicion of moral principles. Feminist philosophers resist the temptation to map out moral actions according to moral principles. Whereas Kant wants to reduce all moral deliberation to adherence to a single rule (the categorical imperative), feminists demur. They argue that principles such as autonomy, justice, and utility are too general and too unwieldy to be of much use in the complicated, multifaceted arena of the domestic, social, and personal. The principle of autonomy may tell a woman she has freedom of choice, but it has nothing to say about her particular situation and the restraints placed on her by her poverty, culture, religion, upbringing, male relatives, social expectations, financial dependence on her husband or other males, and overwhelming domestic duties.

The rejection of impartiality. Recall that the principle of impartiality is regarded as a defining characteristic of morality itself. Impartiality says that from the moral point of view, all persons are considered equal and should be treated accordingly. But in the domestic sphere we are anything but impartial. We are naturally partial to the people we care about—our family and friends. Typically we would not think of treating our spouse the same way we treat a store clerk or the bus driver. We have moral duties to the former that we do not have to the latter. Feminist ethics tries to take these duties into account instead of ignoring them as Kant and Mill would have us do.

A greater respect for emotions. As we've seen, Kant has no place for emotions in his theory. Reading our moral duties off the categorical imperative is all that is required. But in feminist ethics, emotions play a larger role. Feminist ethics is more comfortable with moral guides in the form of virtues rather than rules (see the next chapter on virtue ethics), and the cornerstones of the ethics of care are not rules but feelings. Moral philosophers of all stripes recognize the importance of emotions. They understand that emotions can alert us to moral evil, provide the motivation to pursue the good, and enable us to empathize with the suffering of others. (Moral philosophers also caution that feelings without thinking are blind, and thinking without feelings makes for a sterile morality.)

THE ETHICS OF CARE

The **ethics of care** is a good example of feminist ethics. It is a perspective on moral issues that emphasizes close personal relationships and moral virtues such as compassion, faithfulness, kindness, love, and sympathy. It contrasts dramatically with traditional moral theories preoccupied with principles and legalistic moral reasoning.

Much of the interest in the ethics of care was sparked by research done by the psychologist Carol Gilligan on how men and women think about moral problems.[3] She maintains that men and women think in radically different ways when making moral decisions. According to Gilligan, in moral decision making, men deliberate about rights, justice, and rules; women, on the other hand, focus on personal relationships, caring for others, and being aware of people's feelings, needs, and viewpoints. She dubbed these two approaches the *ethic of justice* and the *ethic of care*.

More recent research has raised doubts about whether there really is a gap between the moral thinking styles of men and women. But these findings do not dilute the relevance of caring to ethics. The ethics of care, regardless of any empirical underpinnings, is a reminder that caring is a vital and inescapable part of the moral life—a conclusion that few philosophers would deny. If virtues are a part of the moral life (as they surely are), and if caring (or compassion, sympathy, or love) is a virtue, then there must be a place for caring alongside principles of moral conduct and moral reasoning. The philosopher Annette C. Baier, an early proponent of the ethics of care, makes a case for both care and justice: "It is clear, I think, that the best moral theory has to be a cooperative product of women and men, has to harmonize justice and care. The morality it theorizes about is after all for all persons, for men and women, and will need their combined insights."[4]

Here is the feminist philosopher Virginia Held explaining the need for care in the moral life:

> First, the central focus of the ethics of care is on the compelling moral salience of attending to and meeting the needs of the particular others for whom we take responsibility. Caring for one's child, for instance, may well and defensibly be at the forefront of a person's moral concerns. The ethics of care recognizes that human beings are dependent for many years of their lives, that the moral claim of those dependent on us for the care they need is pressing, and that there are highly important moral aspects in developing the relations of caring that enable human beings to live and progress. All persons need care for at least their early years. Prospects for human progress and flourishing hinge fundamentally on the care that those needing it receive, and the ethics of care stresses the moral force of the responsibility to respond to the needs of the dependent. Many persons will become ill and dependent for some periods of their later lives, including in frail old age, and some who are permanently disabled will need care the whole of their lives. Moralities built on the image of the independent, autonomous, rational individual largely overlook the reality of human dependence and the morality for which it calls. The ethics of care attends to this central concern of human life and delineates the moral values involved. It refuses to relegate care to a realm "outside morality."[5]

KEYWORDS

ethics of care—A perspective on moral issues that emphasizes close personal relationships and moral virtues such as compassion, love, and sympathy.

feminist ethics—An approach to ethics focused on women's interests and experiences and devoted to supporting the moral equality of women and men.

EXERCISES

Review Questions

1. How does feminist ethics differ from Kantian ethics?
2. What attitudes did many of the great ethical theorists have toward women?
3. What ways of feeling and thinking have been regarded in the West as characteristic of women?

4. What kinds of moral issues are more likely to arise from women's experiences than men's?
5. What elements of the moral life does feminist ethics emphasize? What elements does it deemphasize?
6. Why do feminist philosophers think an ethics of care is needed?
7. What are the hard facts that have helped to propel the rise of feminist ethics?
8. What are some of the fundamental elements of the ethics of care?
9. What is Annette Baier's claim about care and justice?
10. What is Carol Gilligan's thesis about moral thinking?

Essay Questions

1. What features of feminist ethics do you find most plausible? Why?
2. Do you think moral principles such as justice and rights have a place in any good moral theory? Why or why not?
3. What part do you think emotions should play in morality?
4. Do you believe there are innate differences in the ways men and women deliberate about moral issues? Or do you think any differences are the result of cultural influences? Explain.
5. Do you believe there are situations in which impartiality is important in moral reasoning? If not, why not? If so, give an example.
6. Suppose you have an opportunity to (1) send $800 to Africa to save a dozen people from starvation or (2) give the money to your little sister to buy books for college. Which would you do? Why?
7. What is the feminist ethics attitude toward moral principles? Compare it to Kant's view.
8. Are there instances of moral decision making in which moral impartiality is not appropriate? Explain.

ETHICAL DILEMMAS

Explain how feminist ethics or the ethics of care could be applied in the following scenarios to determine the proper course of action.

1. Suppose your best friend is in the hospital battling a serious illness and would deeply appreciate a visit from you. But you are also on spring break and, after a very stressful semester, need to forget about all your commitments and just relax. What might the ethics of care have you do? What is a utilitarian likely to do?
2. You want to help your brother overcome a serious addiction to drugs. You know that since he is a member of your family, you have a duty to

help him. But your main reason for trying to help is that you love him and care what happens to him. Which of these two motivating factors (duty and love) would Kant approve of and which would he reject? How might the attitude of someone who embraces feminist ethics differ from Kant's response?

3. Imagine that your town has been hit by a tornado, and you are in a position to rescue only one of a dozen people who are nearby and trapped in demolished houses. The victim who happens to be far-thest from you, but still reachable, is your mother. Which of these twelve people should you rescue? Who would you rescue if feminist ethics was your preferred moral outlook? Who would you rescue if you were a strict act-utilitarian?

Endnotes

1. Alison M. Jaggar, "Feminist Ethics," *Encyclopedia of Ethics,* ed. Lawrence C. Becker and Charlotte B. Becker (New York: Garland, 1992), 361–70.

2. Jaggar, "Feminist Ethics," 363–64.

3. Carol Gilligan, *In a Different Voice: Psychological Theory and Women's Development* (Cambridge, MA: Harvard University Press, 1982).

4. Annette C. Baier, "The Need for More Than Justice," *Canadian Journal of Philosophy,* suppl. vol. 13 (1988): 56.

5. Virginia Held, *The Ethics of Care* (Oxford: Oxford University Press, 2006), 10–13.

CHAPTER 11

Virtue Ethics

Consequentialist moral theories are concerned with the consequences of actions, for the consequences determine the moral rightness of conduct. The production of good over evil is the essence of morality. Nonconsequentialist moral theories are concerned with the moral nature of actions, for the right-making characteristics of actions determine the rightness of conduct. Virtue ethics, however, takes a different turn. **Virtue ethics** is a theory of morality that makes virtue the central concern. When confronted with a moral problem, a utilitarian or a Kantian theorist asks, "What should I *do*?" But a virtue ethicist asks, in effect, "What should I *be*?" For the former, moral conduct is primarily a matter of following or applying a moral principle or rule to a particular situation, and morality is mainly duty-based. For the latter, moral conduct is something that emanates from a person's moral virtues—from his or her moral character—not from obedience to moral laws. In this chapter we try to understand both the main attractions and the major criticisms of this virtue-centered approach to ethics and the moral life.

Most modern virtue ethicists trace their theoretical roots back to the ancients, most notably to Aristotle (384–322 B.C.E.). His ethics is a coherent, virtue-based view that interlocks with his broader philosophical concerns—his theories about causation, society, self, education, mind, and metaphysics. Aristotle says the moral life consists not in following moral rules that stipulate right actions but in striving to be a particular kind of person—a virtuous person whose actions stem naturally from virtuous character.

For Aristotle, every living being has an end toward which it naturally aims. Life is teleological; it is meant not just to *be* something but to *aspire toward* something, to fulfill its proper function. What is the proper aim of human beings? Aristotle argues that the true goal of humans—their greatest good—is **eudaimonia,** which means "happiness" or "flourishing" and refers to the full realization of the good life. To achieve *eudaimonia,* human beings must fulfill the function that is natural and distinctive to them: living fully in accordance with reason. The life of reason entails a life of virtue because the virtues themselves are rational modes of behaving. Thus Aristotle says, "Happiness is an activity of the soul in accordance with complete or perfect virtue." The virtuous life both helps human beings *achieve* true happiness and *is the realization of* true happiness. Virtues make you good, *and* they help you have a good life.

A **virtue** is a stable disposition to act and feel according to some ideal or model of excellence. It is a deeply embedded character trait that can affect actions in countless situations. Aristotle distinguishes between intellectual and moral virtues. Intellectual virtues include wisdom, prudence, rationality, and the like. Moral virtues include fairness, benevolence, honesty, loyalty, conscientiousness, and courage. Aristotle believes that intellectual virtues can be taught, just as logic and mathematics can be taught. But moral virtues can be learned only through practice:

> [M]oral virtue comes about as a result of habit. . . . From this it is also plain that none of the moral virtues arises in us by nature. . . . [B]ut the virtues we get by first exercising them, as also happens in the case of the arts as well. For the things we have to learn before we can do them, we learn by doing them, e.g. men become builders by building and lyreplayers by playing the lyre; so too we become just by doing just acts, temperate by doing temperate acts, brave by doing brave acts.[1]

Aristotle's notion of a moral virtue is what he calls the "**Golden Mean,**" a balance between two behavioral extremes. A moral virtue (courage, for example) is the midpoint between excess (an excess of courage, or foolhardiness) and deficit (a deficit of courage, or cowardice). For Aristotle, then, the virtuous—and happy—life is a life of moderation in all things.

Modern virtue ethicists follow Aristotle's lead in many respects. Some thinkers take issue with his teleological theory of human nature and his concept of a virtue as a mean between opposing tendencies.

And some have offered interesting alternatives to his virtue ethics. But almost all virtue theories owe a debt to Aristotle in one way or another.

Like Aristotle, contemporary thinkers put the emphasis on quality of character and virtues (character traits), rather than on adherence to particular principles or rules of right action. They are concerned with doing the right thing, of course, but moral obligations are derived from virtues. Virtue ethicists are, for example, less likely to ask whether lying is wrong in a particular situation than whether the action or person is honest or dishonest, or whether honesty precludes lying in this case, or whether an exemplar of honesty (say, Gandhi or Jesus) would lie in these same circumstances.

Contemporary virtue ethicists are also Aristotelian in believing that a pure duty-based morality of rule adherence represents a barren, one-dimensional conception of the moral life. First, they agree with Aristotle that the cultivation of virtues is not merely a moral requirement—it is a way (some would say the *only* way) to ensure human flourishing and the good life. Second, they maintain that a full-blown ethics must take into account motives, feelings, intentions, and moral wisdom—factors that they think duty-based morality neglects. This view contrasts dramatically with Kant's duty-based ethics. He argues that to act morally is simply to act out of duty—that is, to do our duty *because* it is our duty. We need not act out of friendship, loyalty, kindness, love, or sympathy. But in virtue ethics, acting from such motivations is a crucial part of acting from a virtuous character, for virtues are stable dispositions that naturally include motivations and feelings. Contrast the action of someone who methodically aids his sick mother solely out of a sense of duty with the person who tends to her mother out of sympathy, love, and loyalty (perhaps in addition to a sense of duty). Most people would probably think that the latter is a better model of the moral life, while the former seems incomplete.

VIRTUE IN ACTION

If moral rules are secondary in virtue ethics, how does a virtue ethicist make moral decisions or guide his or her conduct or judge the behavior of others? Suppose Helen, a conscientious practitioner of Aristotelian virtue ethics, hears William lie to a friend to avoid paying a debt. She does not have to appeal to a moral rule such as "Do not lie" to know that William's action is an instance of dishonesty (or untruthfulness) and that William himself is dishonest. She can see by his actions that he lacks the virtue of honesty.

But to Helen, honesty is more than just a character trait: it is also an essential part of human happiness and flourishing. In her case, honesty is a virtue that she has cultivated for years by behaving honestly and truthfully in a variety of situations (not just in cases of lying). She has taken such trouble in part because cultivating this virtue has helped her become the kind of person she wants to be. She has developed the disposition to act honestly; acting honestly is part of who she is. She sometimes relies on moral rules (or moral rules of thumb) to make moral decisions, but she usually does not need them, because her actions naturally reflect her virtuous character.

In addition, Helen's trained virtues not only guide her actions, but they also inspire the motivations and feelings appropriate to those actions. Helen avoids dishonest dealings, and she does so because this is what a virtuous person would do, because she has compassion and sympathy for innocent people who are cheated, and because dishonesty is not conducive to human happiness and flourishing.

What guidance can Helen obtain in her strivings toward a moral ideal? Like most virtue ethicists, she looks to moral exemplars—people who embody the virtues and inspire others to follow in their steps. (For exemplars of honesty, Helen has several moral heroes to choose from—Socrates, Gandhi, Jesus, the Buddha, Thomas Aquinas, and many others.) As the philosopher Louis Pojman says of virtue systems,

> The primary focus is not on abstract reason but on ideal types of persons or on actual ideal persons. Discovering the proper moral example and imitating that person or ideal type thus replace casuistic reason as the most significant aspects of the moral life. Eventually, the apprentice-like training in virtue gained by imitating the ideal model results in a virtuous person who spontaneously does what is good.[2]

EVALUATING VIRTUE ETHICS

A case can be made for virtue ethics based on how well it seems to explain important aspects of the moral life. Some philosophers, for example, claim that the virtue approach offers a more plausible explanation of the role of motivation in moral actions than duty-based moral systems do. According to Kant's theory, your conduct may be morally acceptable even if you, say, save a friend's life out of a sense of duty alone (that is, without any sincere regard for your friend). But this motivation—your calculating sense of duty—seems a very cold and anemic motivation indeed. Virtue theorists would say that a more natural and morally appropriate response would be to save your friend primarily out of compassion, love, loyalty, or something similar—and these motives are just what we would expect from a virtuous person acting from fully developed virtues.

Some philosophers also remind us that virtue ethics puts primary emphasis on being a good person and living a good life, a life of happiness and flourishing. They say that these aims are obviously central to the moral life and should be part of any adequate theory of morality. Duty-based moral systems, however, pay much less attention to these essential elements.

Many duty-based theorists are willing to concede that there is some truth in both of these claims. They believe that motivation for moral action cannot be derived entirely from considerations of duty, just as appropriate motivation cannot be based solely on virtuous character. And they recognize that the moral life involves more than merely honoring rules and principles. As Aristotle insists, there should be room for moral achievement in morality, for striving toward moral ideals. But even if these claims of the virtue ethicist are true, it does not follow that traditional virtue ethics is the best moral theory or that an ethics without duties or principles is plausible.

Virtue-based ethics seems to meet the minimum requirement of coherence, and it appears to be generally consistent with our commonsense moral judgments and moral experience. Nevertheless critics have taken it to task, with most of the strongest criticisms centering on alleged problems with applying the theory—in other words, with usefulness (Criterion 3).

The critics' main contention is that appeals to virtues or virtuous character without reference to principles of duty cannot give us any useful guidance in deciding what to do. Suppose we are trying to decide what to do when a desperately poor stranger steals money from us. Should we have him arrested? Give him even more money? Ignore the whole affair? According to virtue ethics, we should do what a virtuous person would do, or do what moral exemplars such as Jesus or the Buddha would do, or do what is benevolent or conscientious. But what exactly *would* a virtuous person do? Or what precisely *is* the benevolent or conscientious action? As many philosophers see it, the problem is that virtue ethics says that the right action is the one performed by the virtuous person and that the virtuous person is the one who performs the right action. But this is to argue in a circle and to give us no help in figuring out what to do. To avoid this circularity, they say, we must appeal to some kind of moral standard or principle to evaluate the action itself. Before we can decide if a person is virtuous, we need to judge if her actions are right or wrong—and such judgments take us beyond virtue ethics.

Some argue in a similar vein by pointing out that a person may possess all of the proper virtues and still be unable to tell right from wrong actions. Dr. Z may be benevolent and just but still not know if stem cell research should be continued or stopped, or if he should help a terminal patient commit suicide, or if he should perform a late-term abortion. Likewise, we know that it is possible for a virtuous person to act entirely from virtue and still commit an immoral act. This shows, critics say, that the rightness of actions does not necessarily (or invariably) depend on the content of one's character. We seem to have independent moral standards—independent of character considerations—by which we judge the moral permissibility of actions.

The virtue theorist can respond to these criticisms by asserting that plenty of moral guidance is to be had in statements about virtues and vices. According to virtue ethicist Rosalind Hursthouse,

> [A] great deal of specific action guidance could be found in rules employing the virtue and vice terms ("v-rules") such as "Do what is honest/charitable; do not do what is dishonest/uncharitable." (It is a noteworthy feature of our virtue and vice vocabulary that, although our list of generally recognised virtue terms is comparatively short, our list of vice terms is remarkably, and usefully, long, far exceeding anything that anyone who thinks in terms of standard deontological rules has ever come up with. Much invaluable action guidance comes from avoiding courses of action that would be irresponsible, feckless, lazy, inconsiderate, uncooperative, harsh, intolerant, selfish, mercenary, indiscreet, tactless, arrogant . . . and on and on.)[3]

Hursthouse believes we can discover our moral duties by examining terms that refer to virtues and vices, because moral guidance is implicit in these terms.

Another usefulness criticism crops up because of apparent conflicts between virtues. What should you do if you have to choose between performing or not performing a particular action, and each option involves the same two virtues but in contradictory ways? Suppose your best friend is on trial for murder, and under oath you must testify about what you know of the case, but what you know will incriminate her. The question is, Should you lie? If you lie to save your friend, you will be loyal but dishonest. If you tell the truth, you will be honest but disloyal. The virtues of loyalty and honesty conflict; you simply cannot be both loyal and honest. Virtue ethics says you should act as a virtuous person would. But such advice gives you no guidance on how to do that in this particular case. You need to know which virtue is more important in this situation, but virtue ethics does not seem to provide a useful answer.

The proponent of virtue ethics has a ready reply to this criticism: Some duty-based moral theories, such as Kantian ethics, are also troubled by conflicts (conflicts of rules or principles, for example). Obviously the existence of such conflicts is not a fatal flaw in duty-based ethics, and so it must not be in virtue approaches either. When principles seem to conflict, the duty-based theorist must determine if the conflict is real and, if so, if it can be resolved (by, say, weighting one principle more than another). Virtue ethics, the argument goes, can exercise the same kind of options. Some might observe, however, that incorporating a weighting rule or similar standard into virtue ethics seems to make the theory a blend of duty-based and virtue-based features.

LEARNING FROM VIRTUE ETHICS

Why does the ancient moral tradition of virtue ethics persist—and not just persist but thrive, even enjoying a revival in modern times? Many thinkers would say that virtue ethics is alive and well because it is sustained by an important ethical truth: virtue and character are large, unavoidable constituents of our moral experience. As moral creatures, we regularly judge the moral permissibility of actions *and* assess the goodness of character. If someone commits an immoral act (kills an innocent human being, for example), it matters to us whether the act was committed out of compassion (as in euthanasia), benevolence, loyalty, revenge, rage, or ignorance. The undeniable significance of virtue in morality has obliged many philosophers to consider how best to accommodate virtues into their principle-based theories of morality or to recast those theories entirely to give virtues a larger role.

The rise of virtue ethics has also forced many thinkers to reexamine the place of principles in morality. If we have virtues, do we need principles? Most philosophers would probably say yes and agree with the philosopher William Frankena that "principles without traits [virtues] are impotent and traits without principles are blind":

> To be or to do, that is the question. Should we construe morality as primarily a following of certain principles or as primarily a cultivation of certain dispositions and traits? Must we choose? It is hard to see how a morality of principles can get off the ground except through the development of dispositions to act in accordance with its principles, else all motivation to act on them must be of an *ad hoc* kind, either prudential or impulsively altruistic.[4]

Kant would have us act out of duty alone, granting no bonus points for acting from virtue. Utilitarianism doesn't require, but also doesn't reject, virtuous motives. Yet virtue seems to be as much a part of our moral experience as moral disagreements, moral errors, and moral reasoning. The question is not whether we should care about virtues, but how much we should care and how we can incorporate them into our lives.

KEYWORDS

eudaimonia—Greek for "happiness," or "flourishing."

Golden Mean—Aristotle's notion of a moral virtue as a balance between two behavioral extremes, such as courage and cowardice.

virtue—A stable disposition to act and feel according to some ideal or model of excellence.

virtue ethics—A theory of morality that makes virtue the central concern.

EXERCISES

Review Questions

1. How does virtue ethics differ from duty-based ethics?
2. In what way is Aristotle's virtue ethics considered teleological?
3. What, according to Aristotle, must humans do to achieve *eudaimonia*?
4. Give three examples of moral virtues. Give two examples of intellectual virtues.
5. What important elements do virtue ethicists think are missing from traditional duty-based ethics?
6. How do virtue ethicists use moral exemplars?
7. Does virtue ethics seem to offer a more plausible explanation of the role of motivation in moral actions than does Kantian ethics? If so, how?
8. What is the chief argument against virtue ethics? How can the virtue ethicist respond?
9. What are the strengths and weaknesses of Aristotle's virtue ethics theory?
10. What does Aristotle mean when he says that the virtuous life helps us *achieve* happiness and *is* happiness?

ETHICAL DILEMMAS

Explain how virtue ethics could be applied in the following scenarios to determine the proper course of action.

1. You are walking across town, and a homeless person bumps into you, takes your wallet, and runs away. What would a virtuous person do in this instance? Should the guiding virtue be compassion? fairness? honesty?
2. You are a physician treating a terminally ill woman who is in a great deal of pain that no drug can relieve. She says she has lived a full life and now wants you to end her anguish by helping her die quickly and quietly. She has no known relatives. The American Medical Association's code of ethics absolutely forbids physician-assisted suicide, and the hospital where she is a patient has a similar policy. But you want to alleviate her agony and give her a chance to die with dignity. What would a virtuous person do?
3. Your father has stolen $30,000 from his employer to pay for surgery that his sister desperately needs. Without the surgery, she will be dead

within six months. Only you know about his crime. You also know that no one will ever know who stole the money unless you report the theft to the authorities. Should you turn your father in to the police? Should you keep quiet about the matter? What would a virtuous person do?

Endnotes

1. Aristotle, *Nicomachean Ethics,* trans. W. D. Ross, book II, chapter 1, eBooks@Adelaide, 2004.
2. Louis P. Pojman, *Ethics: Discovering Right and Wrong,* 4th ed. (Belmont, CA: Wadsworth, 2002), 165.
3. Rosalind Hursthouse, "Virtue Ethics," *The Stanford Encyclopedia of Philosophy* (Fall 2003 ed.), ed. Edward N. Zalta, http://plato.stanford. edu/archives/fall2003/entries/ethics-virtue/.
4. William K. Frankena, *Ethics,* 2nd ed. (Englewood Cliffs, NJ: Prentice-Hall, 1973), 65.

CHAPTER 12

A Moral Theory

By now you know that we are all chronic moral theorizers. We can't help ourselves. We usually operate on the ground level of ethics, making judgments about the rightness or wrongness of particular actions or the moral worth of particular people or motives, trying to align our lives with moral norms that we think rest on a solid footing. But sometimes we must take a bird's-eye view of morality to see how these particulars are related, whether they reveal a pattern that informs the moral life, and whether the moral principles we embrace are really worth embracing. In other words, we *theorize*.

In this chapter, I do some of this big-picture theorizing. I try to work out a plausible moral theory of obligation, an explanation of what makes an action right or wrong. I base this theory on what I consider the best aspects of the moral theories discussed earlier and on the elements of the moral life in which we have the greatest confidence.

MORAL COMMON SENSE

As we have seen, the most influential theories of the past—utilitarianism, Kantian ethics, natural law theory, social contract theory, and virtue ethics—offer invaluable moral insights. But each one overlooks at least one feature that seems vital to morality and to any adequate moral theory. Some leave out the consequences of actions, some the claims of autonomy and rights, and some the demands of justice. I think the absence of these elements constitutes a disabling flaw for the theories. But if this assessment is correct—if our best theories to date are not entirely adequate to the task of providing moral guidance and ethical understanding—how can we expect to devise something better? What are our prospects for improving on what we have?

I think our prospects are good. Recall that we are all capable of forming **considered moral judgments**, the assessments we make about cases and principles after careful reflection that is as clear and unbiased as possible. These judgments—what some call our moral common sense—are fallible and revisable, but they can constitute credible evidence in favor of particular judgments or principles. They are used regularly by philosophers not only to formulate principles and theories but also to test them for soundness. When a judgment or principle or theory or value seems questionable, we usually fall back on our most trusted data, our considered judgments.

Our considered judgments tell us that wantonly killing people is wrong, that slavery is a moral abomination, that equals must be treated equally, that respecting the rights of innocent people is morally required, and that inflicting undeserved and unnecessary suffering on others is evil. We are rightly suspicious of any theory that says otherwise. We should have more confidence in our considered judgment that abusing babies is wrong than in any theory that condones it. Of course, our moral common sense can be in error; we can be wrong about what at first seems obvious; and a good moral theory can show us that a considered judgment should be revised. But we are entitled to trust the urgings of common sense unless we have good reasons to doubt them. Utilitarianism, Kantian ethics, natural law theory, social contract theory, and virtue ethics have all been found wanting in large part because they conflict in some way with our considered judgments. Our moral common sense, then, is the starting point of our theorizing as well as the corroboration of what we learn.

BUILDING A MORAL THEORY

Here is one way a moral theory is built: Suppose we begin with our data—our considered judgments rendered about specific cases. We judge that the actions in these cases are morally wrong, and then we look for what these wrong actions have in common. Suppose we notice that all of them share the property of being instances in which people are prevented from exercising their autonomy (their capacity for self-governance). Perhaps a doctor operates on them without their consent, or they are denied their right to live and work where they choose, or they are forced to practice a religion they despise. After much reflection, we think we see a moral principle threading through these cases: people have a right of self-determination. But to avoid jumping to conclusions, we examine many similar cases, and this forces us to modify our principle, perhaps a little bit or perhaps a lot. And our modified principle sheds new light on our cases, perhaps revealing that some of them are not really instances of wrongdoing after all. We gather more considered judgments, and we think they suggest other principles. Ultimately we may conclude that all our principles can be summed up in one dominant principle (as is the case with utilitarianism). Or perhaps we are left with an apparently irreducible set of principles that seem to cover all our moral duties (as in natural law theory). In either situation, we continually test the principles to determine if they lead to reasonable judgments, and we check the plausibility of the judgments by comparing them to the principles. The idea is to eliminate conflicts between the two and try to achieve the closest possible agreement between them. Thus common sense shapes theory, and theory informs common sense.

So in developing a moral theory, we begin with what we know or think we know. And through much critical reflection on our data and the generalizations arising from them, we can formulate a theory, a work in progress, and a more or less useful guide to the moral life.

PRIMA FACIE PRINCIPLES

But what shape would an adequate theory take? The overall structure of a moral theory of obligation depends largely on the number of fundamental principles it has and whether those principles are absolute—that is, whether they are rigid rules that allow no exceptions. Utilitarianism has a single ultimate rule (the principle of utility), and so does Kant's theory (the categorical imperative). For these theories, no principles are more basic. Each basic principle is also absolute; the rule must always be followed in every circumstance. There is no clause that says the rule must be strictly adhered to except in circumstance X or Y. Other theories, however, feature not one but several fundamental principles, which may or may not be absolute. Natural law theory, for example, is based on a handful of absolute rules. But some theories that also contain more than one basic rule reject absolutism.

Of these possible theory configurations, I think only the latter type is plausible. Deep down, we may all want moral principles to be reassuringly sturdy and absolute, but I think this is a false hope. It seems that for any absolute moral principle, we can always find counterexamples in which adhering strictly to the rule can lead to immoral actions and unpalatable results. Recall Kant's example of the poor unfortunate who runs from an insane murderer and hides in a friend's house. When the friend is asked for the whereabouts of the murderer's prey, he has a choice: he can lie and save his friend's life, or he can tell the truth and doom her. Kant thinks he must tell the truth, even if the result is a tragic loss of life. According to Kant, we must do right though the heavens fall. His absolutism compels him to obey the letter of the law. But our considered moral judgments seem to suggest that in situations like this, saving a life is far more important than telling the truth. If the stakes are high enough—if obeying an absolutist rule would cause, say, death and destruction—violating the rule would appear to be the right thing to do.

Our moral common sense also tells us, I think, that there must be more than one basic moral rule that defines our duties. More than one primary rule must be necessary because we obviously have many basic duties, and we cannot derive them all from one another or from one overarching principle. Our duty to benefit others is distinct from our duty to respect their rights; if anything, these are *competing* duties. Theories such as utilitarianism and Kantianism that boast of just one ultimate rule have trouble accounting for these disparate obligations.

Any theory that consists of two or more fundamental rules must explain how the rules relate to one another. For the absolutist, multiple rules lead to a serious problem: they will inevitably produce irresolvable contradictions. Honoring one rule may force the violation of another. Suppose an absolutist theory consists of just two rules: "Care for loved ones in dire need" and "Keep your promises." Suppose you promise to take your mother to see a Broadway show, something she has looked forward to for years, but on that same night your son becomes seriously ill and will suffer horribly if you do not tend to him. If you keep your promise and take your mother to the show, your son will suffer; if you take care of your son, you will break your promise to your mother. You cannot obey one rule without violating the other. In absolutist theories consisting of two or more basic rules, such contradictions are common, and they render the theories implausible. Various attempts have been made by absolutists to answer this kind of criticism, but in my opinion none of these efforts has succeeded or ever will succeed.

I think nonabsolutist, multiple-rule theories have a much better way of dealing with conflicting rules. This approach hinges on the concept of **prima facie principles**—principles that apply in a situation unless exceptions are justified. Exceptions are justified when two rules conflict (when both rules apply but it is not possible to obey both) and one is considered weightier than the other. Viewing the duties in the mother-son case as prima facie would require us to decide which duty was more important and therefore which should be performed. The two rules represent *apparent* duties, but after weighting the duties appropriately, only one constitutes our *actual* duty. This approach to conflicting rules aligns better with our moral common sense: we know that our duties sometimes collide, that a duty can be overridden by a weightier one, and that occasionally we must break the rules in order to do the right thing. We also seem to have a sense that prima facie duties remain fundamentally important even when they are overridden.

So I think that an adequate moral theory, however it is fleshed out, must be based on more than one principle, and the principles should be prima facie (nonabsolute) and irreducible (they cannot be derived from each other).

THREE RULES

The next issue to consider is what these principles are and how they function in the theory. On this point, theories of prima facie principles can differ substantially in both the content of the principles and their number. W. D. Ross (1877–1967), the first philosopher to devise a theory of prima facie duties, thought there were at least seven prima facie duties: duties of *fidelity* (keeping promises, telling the truth); *reparation* (making amends for a wrongful act); *gratitude* (acknowledging services done for us by others); *justice* (distributing benefits and burdens fairly); *beneficence* (benefiting others); *self-improvement* (enhancing our own virtue or intelligence); and *non-maleficence* (not injuring others).[1] More recently, philosophers have tended to argue for a smaller set of prima facie principles—for example, four (autonomy, justice, beneficence, and non-maleficence), or two (justice and beneficence).

These variations may seem to make the task of developing an acceptable theory fairly complex, but the job is actually simpler than it might initially appear. First, principles that may seem fundamental can often be subsumed under fewer, more basic principles, with the highest-level principles supporting subordinate ones. Second, the flawed theories of the past have helped us see that the moral life is defined by a relatively small number of general norms or core values. We have learned from utilitarianism and other consequentialist theories that any plausible moral theory must take into account the effects of actions and the demands of beneficence and non-maleficence, and we have seen in Kant and other nonconsequentialist views the supreme importance of autonomy, rights, and justice. For most theorists, these concerns define the full spectrum of moral norms that inform the moral life. Although philosophers have parsed these general norms in different ways, there is plenty of agreement about what they are.

If all of this is correct, then a satisfactory moral theory that reflects the facts of the moral life should comprise a small number of prima facie principles covering all of the duties endorsed by our considered judgments. Absolutist rules and a structure dominated by a single sovereign principle cannot be features of this theory.

With these requirements in mind, I want to argue for a theory that rests on three prima facie principles: respect, justice, and beneficence. These three, I think, can cover all our basic moral duties while simplifying the process of identifying and weighing obligations. For particular cases, we would have to specify how, and to what, the principles should be applied, but this process is a necessity for any theory of general norms. As is the case with all theories consisting of more than one moral norm, the principles will often conflict. As suggested earlier, the tension is resolved by weighing and balancing the prima facie principles to ascertain actual duties—our "all things considered" obligations.

Respect refers to respect for persons, the guiding value of Kantian ethics and other nonconsequentialist theories. Respect is owed all persons equally because they have intrinsic worth and dignity due to their autonomy—that is, to their capacity for rational decisions, autonomous action, and moral choices. Kant made this point by insisting that we must always treat persons as ends in themselves, never merely as a means to an end (a tool to be used for someone else's purposes). Another way to express this is to say that, as persons, we have *rights*—specifically, **negative rights**, which obligate others not to interfere with our obtaining something. (In my theoretical scheme, **positive rights**—the rights that obligate others to help us obtain something—fall under the principle of beneficence.) Persons have the right not to be treated in certain ways: not to be used or regarded as if they were mere instruments, and not to have their autonomous actions and free choices thwarted or constrained. The principle of respect therefore would prohibit, among other things, lying to persons, cheating them, coercing them, falsely imprisoning them, and manipulating them.

This principle of respect can accommodate most of Ross's prima facie duties. It supports what he calls duties of fidelity, reparation, gratitude, and self-improvement. We can view this latter duty as an obligation to respect ourselves, to more fully develop those capacities that make us persons.

Duties of respect can override the moral weight of an action's consequences. In general, we may not violate the rights of persons, even if the violation would benefit them or others. We would likely condemn a policy that mandated discrimination against a minority just so the majority could be happy. We would not countenance medical experiments on people without their knowledge and consent—even if the experiments were needed to search for a cancer cure.

Respect, however, does not always trump utility. It is, after all, a *prima facie* duty. In some cases we might be justified in flouting the principle of respect, but we would need very strong reasons to do so. For example, if by jailing an innocent person we could thwart a terrorist attack that would kill a thousand people, we most likely would favor jailing the person. From a moral standpoint, the loss of so many lives seems far more important than the injustice of false imprisonment.

The principle of *justice* requires that persons be treated fairly and that they get what is due them. **Retributive justice** concerns the fair use of punishment for wrongdoing. **Distributive justice** (what I will focus on here) is about the fair distribution of society's benefits and costs (such as income, privileges, taxes, health care, jobs, and public service). The essence of this principle is that equals must be treated equally. A rule that applies to someone in a particular situation must apply to anyone else in a relevantly similar situation. Justice, then, reflects a central fact about the moral life: morality requires impartiality. Racial discrimination is contrary to justice because it treats one group differently than it does another, even though no morally relevant differences exist between them.

Like the principle of respect, the justice principle generally overrides concerns about consequences. In fact, one of the strongest criticisms of utilitarianism is that its emphasis on maximizing happiness or welfare is often at odds with our considered judgments about justice. Justice demands equal treatment of persons, but utilitarianism seeks to produce the best balance of good over evil, which may or may not amount to the equal treatment of equals.

I think the proper way to take consequences into account is through the prima facie principle of *beneficence*. This principle is about the good and bad effects of actions, the nonmoral consequences of what we do or don't do. It says we have a qualified duty to benefit others and to avoid causing them harm. This obligation has three different dimensions: (1) we should not deliberately harm others (should not kill, hurt, disable, rob, or terrorize them, for example); (2) we should act to benefit others (to prevent harm or evil, remove harm or evil, and promote good); and (3) we should strive to produce the most favorable balance of good over evil effects, everyone considered (the utilitarian standard). It is possible to view these three options as separate principles in their own right, but I think this approach would muddle the essential difference between our first two principles (respect and justice) and beneficence because the former are not primarily concerned with the consequences of actions, but the latter is.

In some cases we may see that only one element of beneficence is relevant, either Option 1 or Option 2. But often *both* of these options apply, and when considering whether to benefit or not to harm, we must decide which duty is weightier. Either consideration may override any obligation to maximize utility. Suppose a physician wants to try an experimental treatment that will possibly cure a patient's disease but will also cause permanent damage to her lungs. The overriding principle would be to not cause such harm, even if the benefit to be gained is substantial. A third possibility is that both principles apply, and each duty comes with costs and benefits. We then must make a utilitarian calculation (Option 3) to determine the best solution.

The prohibition against deliberately harming others is a common feature in many moral theories: intentionally harming people is always deemed prima facie wrong. This duty calls not for some action, but for *not* performing an action. In most interactions with others, we have an implicit duty not to harm them, but not necessarily a duty to benefit them or to maximize their welfare. If we are driving a heavy truck on a busy highway, for example, our strongest duty is likely to be to refrain from intentionally or carelessly harming other drivers and pedestrians, while we may not have an obligation to benefit them (by, say, continually yielding the right of way to them). And we would not ordinarily have a duty to maximize their good.

It seems that our duty to benefit others (prevent harm, remove harm, and promote good) does not demand that we help *all* persons. Our considered judgments tell us that we may have an obligation to promote the welfare of our family, friends, and others we are close to, but we do not have an equally strong duty to help the rest of the world. Treating everyone with such beneficence would not be the fulfillment of a duty but the performance of a supererogatory act (above the call of duty). We might have a duty to help those in the rest of the world, but that duty cannot be as weighty as the one we have to our loved ones.

We are also not obliged to make *extreme* sacrifices to help those with whom we have no relationship. The principle of beneficence, for example, does not insist that we risk our lives and our health to aid a stranger.

Nevertheless I think we may have at least a limited obligation to help those with whom we have no connection. We surely must sometimes have a "duty of rescue"—an obligation to try to save a stranger in serious peril when we have the wherewithal to save him without extreme risk or cost to ourselves. If we could easily save a drowning man without too much risk or trouble to ourselves, we may be obligated to do so. And if we have such a duty of rescue, we may have other duties of beneficence in morally equivalent circumstances.

Because my proposed theory consists of principles that are prima facie, conflicts among them are less of a problem than they are in absolutist views. Much of the time, weighing and balancing principles to determine our actual duties is straightforward, though sometimes difficult. In each situation that calls for a moral judgment, the basic pattern of our deliberations is something like this: (1) we discern which principles (respect, justice, and beneficence) apply; (2) we weigh them according to their importance in the case; (3) we determine which principle dominates; and (4) we decide what action best fits with this analysis.

The most challenging part of this process is determining the weight of the basic principles. Even if we know what the fundamental principles are, we still have to figure out their relative importance in context. But there is no formula or algorithm to help us with this. Even a rough but firm ranking of principles—in which, say, respect would always outweigh justice, and justice would always outweigh beneficence—would be a tremendous help. But there is no such formula or ranking, and there cannot be one, because the relative importance of the principles fluctuates depending on the details of the case. Sometimes justice may carry the most moral weight, sometimes respect or beneficence.

Our only option is to rely on our reason and experience—that is, our considered judgments and the theory that provides the perspective and insight to these judgments. We must work without a net while trying to grasp at answers, and will occasionally fail. But this difficulty of assigning weight to principles, and trying to do so without detailed instructions, is also a feature of other moral theories. And as discussed earlier, in their search for the best theory to explain a set of data, scientists must also decide the importance of divergent criteria—and do it without a precise decision-making formula. These judgments are like the ones that a physician makes when diagnosing a disease in a particular patient. There are usually rules of thumb to follow, but in the end, the physician must use her best judgment to arrive at an answer. Such judgments are not formulaic, but they are rational and far from arbitrary.

SELF-EVIDENCE

As you can see, my proposed theory appeals at every turn to our moral common sense. But some people might ask, "Who says our considered judgments are reliable guides to moral truth? Why should we trust common sense to identify the true moral principles, especially because we know it to be fallible and sometimes unreliable?" For example, in response to the claim that utilitarianism conflicts with our moral common sense, some utilitarians have said, in effect, "That's too bad for common sense."

One facile response to this disparagement of common sense is to ask, "Doesn't every theory ultimately rely on common sense? Isn't the utilitarian's principle of utility itself founded on common sense because the principle is not supported by a more basic principle?"

But I think a more serious defense of moral common sense and our fundamental moral principles is possible. I want to argue, as several contemporary moral theorists do, that many of our basic moral principles are self-evident.[2] I don't have the space here to fully defend this claim, but I can point out a few considerations that support it.

A **self-evident statement** is one that you are justified in believing merely by understanding it. Here are some self-evident assertions: "Whatever has a shape has a size"; "No bachelors are married"; and "If A is larger than B, and B is larger than C, then A is larger than C." If you understand what these statements mean, then you are justified in believing them, and you need no special faculty to discern their truth. You don't need to gather evidence or conduct experiments to know them; you know them as soon as you grasp their meaning (whether you understand them immediately or after long reflection). If someone insists that the statement "No bachelors are married" is not true, it is up to him to provide a counterexample—to cite a circumstance in which the statement would not be true. If he cannot, then he has no reasons supporting his assertion that the statement is false; his assertion is groundless. This is the only kind of response we can make to those who reject beliefs that we consider to be self-evidently true.

I take it that the following are self-evident moral beliefs (which are also prima facie moral principles):

- Equals should be treated equally.
- It is wrong to punish the innocent.
- It is wrong to inflict unnecessary and undeserved suffering.
- It is wrong to torture people for fun.

I have come to know these statements in the same way that I come to know nonmoral truths—through reason and reflection, not by any extraordinary faculties or irrational process.

As in the case of nonmoral statements, if someone thinks that "It is wrong to inflict unnecessary and undeserved suffering" is not true, it is up to her to cite circumstances in which the statement would be false. If she cannot, then her rejection of the principle is unwarranted.

If there are self-evident moral truths, it is reasonable to expect that some of our prima facie principles arising from our considered moral judgments are in fact self-evident. Their self-evidence would explain why we have such confidence in some moral principles—so much confidence that we would sooner give up a theory that denied the principles than the principles themselves. If at least some of my theory's prima facie principles are self-evident, the proposed theory (and theories like it) are on firmer ground than some might think.

The hard truth about moral theorizing is that it never seems to result in a widely accepted, complete, or unblemished theory. My proposal is no exception to the rule. But it does have the advantage of incorporating what I regard as the most manifest and least questionable elements of the moral life.

KEYWORDS

considered moral judgment—A moral assessment that is as free from bias and distorting passions as possible. We generally trust such a judgment unless there is a reason to doubt it.

distributive justice—The fair distribution of society's benefits and costs (such as income, taxes, jobs, and public service).

negative right—A person's right that obligates others not to interfere with that person's obtaining something.

positive right—A person's right that obligates others to help that person obtain something.

prima facie principle—A principle that applies in a situation unless exceptions are justified.

retributive justice—The fair use of punishment for wrongdoing.

self-evident statement—An assertion that a person is justified to believe merely by understanding it, such as "No bachelors are married."

EXERCISES

Review Questions

1. What are considered moral judgments?
2. Why have the previously discussed theories been found wanting?
3. What is a prima facie judgment?
4. What is an absolute principle?
5. Why does the author think there is more than one basic moral principle?
6. Why are conflicts among absolutist principles a problem?

7. What is the difference between an apparent duty and an actual duty?
8. What are the fundamental principles of the author's theory?
9. What is the principle of respect?
10. What are the three dimensions of the beneficence principle?

Essay Questions

1. Do you think the author's theory conforms to moral common sense? Why or why not?
2. What is the difference between negative and positive rights? Why might someone object to positive rights? Do you believe in positive rights? Why or why not?
3. Why is racial discrimination contrary to the principle of justice?
4. Do we have an obligation to make extreme sacrifices to help strangers? Why or why not?
5. How are conflicts among prima facie principles handled?
6. Do you believe we have absolute moral duties? Why or why not?
7. Do you think that "Equals should be treated equally" is a self-evident moral statement? Explain.
8. Do you believe there are any self-evident moral principles at all? Why or why not?

ETHICAL DILEMMAS

Explain how the author's moral theory could be applied in the following scenarios to determine the proper course of action.

1. Your grandmother is near death in the hospital, barely conscious but in great pain. She has terminal cancer, and her medical team assures you that she may linger in this state for a week at most but will never recover. A year ago she made you promise that no matter how much she suffers, you are not to allow anyone to shorten her life by removing her ventilator or by letting her doctors administer "terminal sedation"—medication that relieves pain while slowly ending life (a legal form of euthanasia). You can hardly bear to see her in such agony. Should you keep your promise to her and ensure that she lingers in horrible suffering, or should you break your promise and request terminal sedation or removal of all life support?

2. Your father has been arrested and put on trial for beating—and nearly killing—an immigrant from Southeast Asia, a form of vigilantism that you think he would never participate in. The prosecuting attorney,

bent on ridding society of racially motivated violence, has a weak case so far. But then you find a handwritten letter by your father in which he relates in great detail how he intends to beat the immigrant to death. You are shocked and suddenly aware of a terrible choice you must make. You could turn the letter over to the prosecutor and ensure your father's conviction, or you could destroy it and pave the way for his acquittal. Your loyalty to a member of your family is in conflict with your sense of justice. Which should you choose?

Endnotes

1. W. D. Ross, *The Right and the Good* (Oxford: Oxford University Press, 1930).
2. See, for example, Robert Audi, *Moral Knowledge and Ethical Character* (Oxford: Oxford University Press, 1997); and Russ Shafer-Landau, *Moral Realism: A Defence* (Oxford: Oxford University Press, 2003).

FURTHER READING

CHAPTER 1. Ethics and the Moral Life

Anita L. Allen, *New Ethics: A Guided Tour of the Twenty-First-Century Moral Landscape* (New York: Miramax, 2004).

Aristotle, *Nicomachean Ethics*, Book 2, Parts 1 and 4.

Simon Blackburn, *Being Good: A Short Introduction to Ethics* (Oxford: Oxford University Press, 2002).

Donald M. Borchert and David Stewart, *Exploring Ethics* (New York: Macmillan, 1986).

Steven M. Cahn and Joram G. Haber, eds., *Twentieth Century Ethical Theory* (Englewood Cliffs, NJ: Prentice Hall, 1995).

William K. Frankena, *Ethics*, 2nd ed. (Englewood Cliffs, NJ: Prentice-Hall, 1973).

Bernard Gert, *Morality: Its Nature and Justification* (New York: Oxford University Press, 1998).

Brooke Noel Moore and Robert Michael Stewart, *Moral Philosophy: A Comprehensive Introduction* (Belmont, CA: Mayfield, 1994).

Louis P. Pojman and Lewis Vaughn, eds., *The Moral Life: An Introductory Reader in Ethics and Literature*, 5th ed. (New York: Oxford University Press, 2014).

Dave Robinson and Chris Garrett, *Introducing Ethics*, ed. Richard Appignanesi (New York: Totem Books, 2005).

Peter Singer, ed., *A Companion to Ethics*, corr. ed. (Oxford: Blackwell, 1993).

Paul Taylor, *Principles of Ethics: An Introduction* (Encino, CA: Dickenson, 1975).

Jacques P. Thiroux, *Ethics: Theory and Practice*, 3rd ed. (New York: Macmillan, 1986).

Lewis Vaughn, *Doing Ethics*, 3rd ed. (New York: W. W. Norton, 2013).

Thomas F. Wall, *Thinking Critically about Moral Problems* (Belmont, CA: Wadsworth, 2003).

G. J. Warnock, *The Object of Morality* (London: Methuen, 1971).

CHAPTER 2. Relativism and Emotivism

A. J. Ayer, *Language, Truth and Logic* (1936; reprint, New York: Dover, 1952).

Brand Blanshard, "Emotivism," in *Reason and Goodness* (1961; reprint, New York: G. Allen & Unwin, 1978).

Donald M. Borchert and David Stewart, "Ethical Emotivism," in *Exploring Ethics* (New York: Macmillan, 1986).

Richard B. Brandt, *Ethical Theory: The Problems of Normative and Critical Ethics* (Englewood Cliffs, NJ: Prentice-Hall, 1959), chap. 11.

Jean Bethke Elshtain, "Judge Not?" *First Things*, no. 46 (October 1994): 36–40.

Fred Feldman, *Introductory Ethics* (Englewood Cliffs, NJ: Prentice-Hall, 1978), chap 11.

Chris Gowans, "Moral Relativism," *The Stanford Encyclopedia of Philosophy* (Spring 2004 ed.), ed. Edward N. Zalta, http://plato.stanford.edu/archives/spr2004/ entries/moral-relativism.

Melville Herskovits, *Cultural Relativism: Perspectives in Cultural Pluralism*, ed. Frances Herskovits (New York: Random House, 1972).

J. L. Mackie, *Ethics: Inventing Right and Wrong* (Harmondsworth, UK: Penguin, 1977).

Theodore Schick Jr. and Lewis Vaughn, *Doing Philosophy: An Introduction through Thought Experiments*, 2nd ed. (Boston: McGraw-Hill, 2003), chap. 5.

Peter Singer, ed., *A Companion to Ethics,* corr. ed. (Oxford: Blackwell, 1993), chap. 38, 39.

Walter T. Stace, "Ethical Relativism," in *The Concept of Morals* (1937; reprint, New York: Macmillan, 1965).

Paul Taylor, *Principles of Ethics: An Introduction* (Encino, CA: Dickenson, 1975), chap. 2.

CHAPTER 3. Moral Arguments

Richard Feldman, *Reason and Argument*, 2nd ed. (Upper Saddle River, NJ: Prentice Hall, 1999).

Richard M. Fox and Joseph P. DeMarco, *Moral Reasoning: A Philosophic Approach to Applied Ethics*, 2nd ed. (Fort Worth, TX: Harcourt College Publishers, 2001).

Brooke Noel Moore and Richard Parker, *Critical Thinking*, 7th ed. (Boston: McGraw-Hill, 2004).

Lewis Vaughn, *The Power of Critical Thinking: Effective Reasoning about Ordinary and Extraordinary Claims* (New York: Oxford University Press, 2005).

Lewis Vaughn, *Doing Ethics*, 3rd ed. (New York: W. W. Norton, 2013).

CHAPTER 4. Moral Theories

John D. Arras and Nancy K. Rhoden, "The Need for Ethical Theory," in *Ethical Issues in Modern Medicine*, 3rd ed. (Mountain View, CA: Mayfield, 1989).

Richard B. Brandt, *Ethical Theory: The Problems of Normative and Critical Ethics* (Englewood Cliffs, NJ: Prentice-Hall, 1959).

C. D. Broad, *Five Types of Ethical Theory* (1930; reprint, London: Routledge & Kegan Paul, 1956).

C. E. Harris, *Applying Moral Theories* (Belmont, CA: Wadsworth, 1997).

John Rawls, "Some Remarks about Moral Theory," in *A Theory of Justice*, rev. ed. (Cambridge, MA: Harvard University Press, Belknap Press, 1999).

CHAPTER 5. Ethical Egoism

C. D. Broad, "Egoism as a Theory of Human Motives," in *Twentieth Century Ethical Theory*, ed. Steven M. Cahn and Joram G. Haber (Englewood Cliffs, NJ: Prentice-Hall, 1995).

David Gauthier, ed., *Morality and Rational Self-Interest* (Englewood Cliffs, NJ: Prentice-Hall, 1970).

Louis P. Pojman and Lewis Vaughn, eds., *The Moral Life: An Introductory Reader in Ethics and Literature*, 5th ed. (New York: Oxford University Press, 2014).

Robert Shaver, "Egoism," *The Stanford Encyclopedia of Philosophy*, 2010, http://plato.stanford.edu/entries/egoism/.

Paul W. Taylor, "Ethical Egoism," in *Principles of Ethics: An Introduction* (Encino, CA: Dickenson, 1975).

Richard Taylor, *Good and Evil* (New York: Macmillan, 1970).

CHAPTER 6. Utilitarianism

Jeremy Bentham, "Of the Principle of Utility," in *An Introduction to the Principles of Morals and Legislation* (1789).

Steven M. Cahn and Joram G. Haber, eds., *Twentieth Century Ethical Theory* (Englewood Cliffs, NJ: Prentice-Hall, 1995).

Fred Feldman, "Act Utilitarianism: Pro and Con," in *Introductory Ethics* (Englewood Cliffs, NJ: Prentice-Hall, 1978).

William Frankena, "Utilitarianism, Justice, and Love," in *Ethics*, 2nd ed. (Englewood Cliffs, NJ: Prentice-Hall, 1973).

C. E. Harris, "The Ethics of Utilitarianism," in *Applying Moral Theories*, 3rd ed. (Belmont, CA: Wadsworth, 1997).

Kai Nielsen, "A Defense of Utilitarianism," *Ethics* 82 (1972): 113–24.

J. J. C. Smart, "Extreme and Restricted Utilitarianism," in *Essays Metaphysical and Moral: Selected Philosophical Papers* (Oxford: Blackwell, 1987).

Bernard Williams, "A Critique of Utilitarianism," in *Utilitarianism: For and Against*, ed. J. J. C. Smart and Bernard Williams (Cambridge: Cambridge University Press, 1973).

CHAPTER 7. Kantian Ethics

Harry Acton, *Kant's Moral Theory* (New York: Macmillan, 1970).

C. D. Broad, *Five Types of Ethical Theory* (1930; reprint, London: Routledge & Kegan Paul, 1956).

C. E. Harris, *Applying Moral Theories*, 3rd ed. (Belmont, CA: Wadsworth, 1997), chap. 6, 8.

Onora O'Neill, "Kantian Ethics," in *A Companion to Ethics*, corr. ed., ed. Peter Singer (Oxford: Blackwell, 1993).

W. D. Ross, *Kant's Ethical Theory* (Oxford: Clarendon Press, 1954).
Paul Taylor, *Principles of Ethics: An Introduction* (Encino, CA: Dickenson, 1975), chap. 5.
Robert N. Van Wyk, *Introduction to Ethics* (New York: St. Martin's, 1990), chap. 4, 6.

CHAPTER 8. Natural Law Theory

Stephen Buckle, "Natural Law," in *A Companion to Ethics*, corr. ed., ed. Peter Singer (Oxford: Blackwell, 1993).
John Finnis, *Natural Law and Natural Rights* (Oxford: Clarendon Press; New York: Oxford University Press, 1980).
Mark Murphy, "The Natural Law Tradition in Ethics," *The Stanford Encyclopedia of Philosophy* (Winter 2002 ed.), ed. Edward N. Zalta, http://plato.stanford. edu/ archives/win2002/entries/natural-law-ethics.
Kai Nielsen, *Ethics without God* (London: Pemberton; Buffalo, NY: Prometheus, 1973).
Louis P. Pojman, "Natural Law," in *Ethics: Discovering Right and Wrong*, 4th ed. (Belmont, CA: Wadsworth, 2002).

CHAPTER 9. Social Contract Theory

David Gauthier, ed., *Morality and Rational Self-Interest* (Englewood Cliffs, NJ: Prentice-Hall, 1970).
Thomas Hobbes, *Leviathan,* 1651.
John Hospers, *Human Conduct: Problems of Ethics*, shorter ed. (New York: Harcourt Brace Jovanovich, 1972).
Robert Nozick, *Anarchy, State, and Utopia* (New York: Basic Books, 1974).
John Rawls, *A Theory of Justice* (Cambridge, MA: Harvard University Press, 1999).
John Simmons, *Political Philosophy* (New York: Oxford University Press, 2008).
Jonathan Wolff, *An Introduction to Political Philosophy* (Oxford: Oxford University Press, 2006).

CHAPTER 10. The Feminist Challenge

Carol Gilligan, *In a Different Voice: Psychological Theory and Women's Development* (Cambridge, MA: Harvard University Press, 1982).
Virginia Held, *Feminist Morality: Transforming Culture, Society, and Politics* (Chicago: University of Chicago Press, 1993).
Virginia Held, *The Ethics of Care* (Oxford: Oxford University Press, 2006), 10–13.
Alison M. Jaggar, *Feminist Politics and Human Nature* (Totowa, NJ: Allenheld, 1983).
Alison M. Jaggar, "Feminist Ethics," *Encyclopedia of Ethics*, ed. Lawrence C. Becker and Charlotte B. Becker (New York: Garland, 1992), 361–70.
Martha Nussbaum, "The Feminist Critique of Liberalism," in *Women's Voices, Women's Rights*, ed. A. Jeffries (Boulder, CO: Westview Press, 1999).

Susan Moller Okin, *Justice, Gender, and the Family* (New York: Basic Books, 1989).

Mary Wollstonecraft, *A Vindication of the Rights of Woman*, ed. M. Brody (London: Penguin, 1988).

CHAPTER 11. Virtue Ethics

G. E. M. Anscombe, "Modern Moral Philosophy," *Philosophy* 33, no. 124 (January 1958): 1–19.

Philippa Foot, "Virtues and Vices," in *Virtues and Vices and Other Essays in Moral Philosophy* (Berkeley: University of California Press, 1978).

William K. Frankena, "Ethics of Virtue," in *Ethics*, 2nd ed. (Englewood Cliffs, NJ: Prentice-Hall, 1973).

Rosalind Hursthouse, "Virtue Ethics," *The Stanford Encyclopedia of Philosophy* (Fall 2003 ed.), ed. Edward N. Zalta, http://plato.stanford/archives/fall2003/ entries/ ethics-virtue.

Alasdair MacIntyre, "The Nature of the Virtues," in *After Virtue: A Study in Moral Theory* (Notre Dame, IN: University of Notre Dame Press, 1984).

Greg Pence, "Virtue Theory," in *A Companion to Ethics*, corr. ed., ed. Peter Singer (Oxford: Blackwell, 1993).

CHAPTER 12. A Moral Theory

Robert Audi, *Moral Knowledge and Ethical Character* (Oxford: Oxford University Press, 1997).

William K. Frankena, "Ethics of Virtue," in *Ethics*, 2nd ed. (Englewood Cliffs, NJ: Prentice-Hall, 1973).

C. E. Harris, *Applying Moral Theories*, 3rd ed. (Belmont, CA: Wadsworth, 1997), chap. 6, 8.

John Rawls, "Some Remarks about Moral Theory," in *A Theory of Justice*, rev. ed. (Cambridge, MA: Harvard University Press, Belknap Press, 1999).

W. D. Ross, *Kant's Ethical Theory* (Oxford: Clarendon Press, 1954).

Russ Shafer-Landau, *Moral Realism: A Defence* (Oxford: Oxford University Press, 2003).

GLOSSARY

act-egoism—The theory that to determine right action, you must apply the egoistic principle to individual acts.

act-utilitarianism—The theory that morally right actions are those that directly produce the greatest overall good, everyone considered.

appeal to authority—The fallacy of relying on the opinion of someone thought to be an expert who is not.

appeal to emotion—The fallacy of trying to convince someone to accept a conclusion by appealing only to fear, guilt, anger, hate, compassion, and the like.

appeal to ignorance—The fallacy of arguing that the absence of evidence entitles us to believe a claim.

appeal to the person—The fallacy (also known as *ad hominem*) of arguing that a claim should be rejected solely because of the characteristics of the person who makes it.

applied ethics—The application of moral norms to specific moral issues or cases, particularly those in a profession such as medicine or law.

argument—A group of statements, one of which is supposed to be supported by the rest.

begging the question—The fallacy of arguing in a circle—that is, trying to use a statement as both a premise in an argument and the conclusion of that argument. Such an argument says, in effect, *p* is true because *p* is true.

categorical imperative—A command that we should follow regardless of our particular wants and needs; also, the single principle that defines Kant's ethical system, from which all additional maxims can be derived.

cogent argument—A strong argument with true premises.

conclusion—The statement supported in an argument.

consequentialist theory—A moral theory asserting that what makes an action right is its consequences.

considered moral judgment—A moral assessment that is as free from bias and distorting passions as possible. We generally trust such a judgment unless there is a reason to doubt it.

cultural relativism—The view that an action is morally right if one's culture approves of it.

deductive argument—An argument that is supposed to give logically conclusive support to its conclusion.

deontologist—One who believes that the rightness of an action derives not from the consequences of an action but from its nature (its right-making characteristics).

descriptive ethics—The scientific study of moral beliefs and practices.

distributive justice—The fair distribution of society's benefits and costs (such as income, taxes, jobs, and public service).

divine command theory—A theory asserting that the morally right action is the one that God commands.

doctrine of double effect—The principle that performing a good action may be permissible even if it has bad effects, but performing a bad action for the purpose of achieving good effects is never permissible; any bad effects must be unintended.

emotivism—The view that moral utterances are neither true nor false but are expressions of emotions or attitudes.

equivocation—The fallacy of assigning two different meanings to the same term in an argument.

ethical egoism—The theory that the morally right action is the one that advances one's own best interests.

ethics (or *moral philosophy*)—The philosophical study of morality.

ethics of care—A perspective on moral issues that emphasizes close personal relationships and moral virtues such as compassion, love, and sympathy.

eudaimonia—Greek for "happiness," or "flourishing."

extrinsically valuable—Valuable as a means to something else, such as the pen that can be used to write a letter.

fallacy—A common but faulty argument.

faulty analogy—The use of a flawed analogy to argue for a conclusion.

feminist ethics—An approach to ethics focused on women's interests and experiences and devoted to supporting the moral equality of women and men.

Golden Mean—Aristotle's notion of a moral virtue as a balance between two behavioral extremes, such as courage and cowardice.

greatest happiness principle—According to John Stuart Mill, the principle that "holds that actions are right in proportion as they tend to promote happiness, wrong as they tend to produce the reverse of happiness."

hasty generalization—The fallacy of drawing a conclusion about an entire group of people or things based on an undersized sample of the group.

hypothetical imperative—A command that tells us what we should do if we have certain desires.

hypothetical syllogism—An argument of the form: If p, then q; if q, then r; therefore, if p, then r.

imperfect duty—A duty that has exceptions.

indicator words—Terms that often appear in arguments to signal the presence of a premise or conclusion, or to indicate that an argument is deductive or inductive.

inductive argument—An argument that is supposed to offer probable support to its conclusion.

intrinsically valuable—Valuable in itself, for its own sake, such as happiness or beauty.

invalid argument—A deductive argument that does not offer logically conclusive support for the conclusion.

Kant's theory—A theory asserting that the morally right action is the one done in accordance with the categorical imperative.

means-ends principle—The rule that we must always treat people (including ourselves) as ends in themselves, never merely as a means.

metaethics—The study of the meaning and logical structure of moral beliefs.

modus ponens—An argument of the form: If *p*, then *q*; *p*; therefore, *q*.

modus tollens—An argument of the form: If *p*, then *q*; not *q*; therefore, not *p*.

morality—Beliefs concerning right and wrong, good and bad; they can include judgments, rules, principles, and theories.

moral statement—A statement affirming that an action is right or wrong or that a person (or one's motive or character) is good or bad.

moral theory—An explanation of what makes an action right or what makes a person or thing good.

natural law theory—A theory asserting that the morally right action is the one that follows the dictates of nature.

negative right—A person's right that obligates others not to interfere with that person's obtaining something.

nonconsequentialist theory—A moral theory asserting that the rightness of an action does not depend on its consequences.

nonmoral statement—A statement that does not affirm that an action is right or wrong or that a person (or one's motive or character) is good or bad.

normative ethics—The study of the principles, rules, or theories that guide our actions and judgments.

objectivism—The view that some moral principles are valid for everyone.

perfect duty—A duty that has no exceptions.

positive right—A person's right that obligates others to help that person obtain something.

premise—A supporting statement in an argument.

prima facie principle—A principle that applies in a situation unless exceptions are justified.

principle of utility—Jeremy Bentham's "principle which approves or disapproves of every action whatsoever, according to the tendency which it appears to have to augment or diminish the happiness of the party whose interest is in question."

psychological egoism—The scientific view that the motive for all our actions is self-interest.

retributive justice—The fair use of punishment for wrongdoing.

rule-egoism—The theory that to determine right action, you must see if an act falls under a rule that if consistently followed would maximize your self-interest.

rule-utilitarianism—The theory that the morally right action is the one covered by a rule that if generally followed would produce the most favorable balance of good over evil, everyone considered.

self-evident statement—An assertion that a person is justified to believe merely by understanding it, such as "No bachelors are married."

slippery slope—The fallacy of using dubious premises to argue that doing a particular action will inevitably lead to other actions that will result in disaster, so you should not do the first action.

social contract theory—The doctrine that morality arises from a social contract that self-interested and rational people would abide by in order to secure a degree of peace, prosperity, and safety.

sound argument—A valid argument with true premises.

statement—An assertion that something is or is not the case. Also called a *claim*.

straw man—The fallacy of misrepresenting someone's claim or argument so it can be more easily refuted.

strong argument—An inductive argument that provides probable support for its conclusion.

subjective relativism—The view that an action is morally right if one approves of it.

supererogatory actions—Conduct that is "above and beyond" duty; not required, but praiseworthy.

utilitarianism—A theory asserting that the morally right action is the one that produces the most favorable balance of good over evil, everyone considered.

valid argument—A deductive argument that provides logically conclusive support for its conclusion.

virtue—A stable disposition to act and feel according to some ideal or model of excellence.

virtue ethics—A theory of morality that makes virtue the central concern.

weak argument—An inductive argument that does not give probable support to its conclusion.

INDEX

A

absolutism, 29
  categorical imperative and, 83, 122,
    126–27
  moral theory and, 170, 173–74
  natural law theory and, 84, 134–35,
    137–38
  prima facie principles and, 167–69
act-egoism, 93, 94–95
act-utilitarianism, 82, 104–8, 109–16,
  125
adequacy, moral criteria of, 85–89,
  99–101
ad hominem fallacy, 71–72
appeal to authority fallacy, 68
appeal to emotion fallacy, 69
appeal to ignorance fallacy, 70–71
appeal to the person fallacy, 71–72
applied ethics, 17
Aquinas, Thomas, 24, 132–35. *See also*
  natural law theory
arguments. *See* moral arguments
Aristotle, 155–57, 159
Asch, Solomon, 36
assertion, in logical argument, 19
Ayer, A. J., 40–41

B

Baier, Annette C., 151–52
begging the question fallacy, 67
beneficence, 117, 170, 172–74
Bentham, Jeremy, 104–7, 110–11
Blanshard, Brand, 43

Broad, C. D., 128
Brothers Karamazov (Dostoyevsky), 24

C

care, ethics of, 151–52
categorical imperative, 83, 120–31,
  141, 168, 171
  basics and applications of, 122–26
  evaluation of, 126–29
  virtue ethics contrasted, 157, 159,
    161, 162
  see also Kant, Immanuel
cogent argument, 53
cognitivism, 40
coherence, moral theory and, 85, 99,
  111, 116, 126, 159
conclusions, in critical reasoning, 19,
  48–53, 59–66
conditional argument, 53–54
consequentialist (teleological) moral
  theories, 81–82, 120, 155
conservatism, moral theory and, 86
considered moral judgments, 64, 80
  moral theory development and,
    166–67, 174–75
  see also consistency, with considered
    judgments (Criterion 1)
consistency, with considered
  judgments (Criterion 1), 86–87
  categorical imperative and, 126, 128
  ethical egoism and, 99–100
  natural law theory and, 136–38
  utilitarianism and, 111–14

ısistency, with moral experience
(Criterion 2), 87–88
categorical imperative and, 126–27
ethical egoism and, 100
natural law theory and, 135–36
utilitarianism and, 114–15
contractarianism. *See* social contract
theory
counterexamples, arguments and,
55–56, 63
critical reasoning
basics of, 46–58
as element of ethics, 16, 17, 19
emotivism and, 41–42
neutral standard and, 23
cultural relativism, 30, 32–40

D

deductive arguments, 51–56
deontology. *See* nonconsequentialist
moral theories
descriptive ethics, 16–17
disagreements, moral
cultural relativism and, 37–38
emotivism and, 41
subjective relativism and, 32
distributive justice, 171–72
divine command theory, 24–25, 84, 141
Dostoyevsky, Fyodor, 24
double effect, doctrine of, 134–36

E

emotivism, 30, 40–43
Epicurus, 93
equivocation fallacy, 67–68
ethical egoism, 92–102, 105, 129
basics and applications of, 82, 92–96
evaluation of, 96–101
ethics (moral philosophy), 13–28
divisions of, 17–18
elements of, 18–21
necessity of "doing," 13–16
religion and, 21–25
eudaimonia, 156
Euthyphro (Socrates), 24
experience. *See* consistency, with moral
experience (Criterion 2)
extrinsic value, 18

F

fallacies, 66–72
faulty analogy fallacy, 69–70
Feinberg, Joel, 98
feminist ethics, 148–54
Frankena, William, 162
fruitfulness, moral theory and, 86

G

Gilligan, Carol, 151
Golden Mean, 156
greatest happiness principle, 105

H

happiness, utilitarianism and, 104–8,
111–14
hasty generalization fallacy, 72
hedonic calculus, 106
Held, Virginia, 152
Hobbes, Thomas, 142–44
Hursthouse, Rosalind, 160–61
hypothetical imperative, 121–22
hypothetical syllogism, 55

I

impartiality, principle of, 20–21
categorical imperative, 129
ethical egoism and, 100
feminist rejection of, 150
utilitarianism and, 117
imperfect duties, 122
indicator words, in arguments, 50,
52
inductive argument, 51–56
infallibility, realism and, 31–32, 37,
39
intellectual virtues, 156
intention, natural law theory, 138–39
intrinsic value, 18
invalid argument, 51–56, 62

J

Jaggar, Alison M., 148–49
justice, 115, 170, 171–72

K

Kant, Immanuel, 83, 120–21. *See also*
categorical imperative

L

Leibniz, Gottfried, 24–25
Leviathan (Hobbes), 142–44
logic, 16, 19. *See also* moral arguments

M

McCloskey, H. J., 111
means-ends principle, 124–25, 126, 128–29
metaethics, 17
Mill, John Stuart, 14–15, 104–7, 110–11, 117
modus ponens/modus tollens, 54–55
moral arguments, 46–77
  critical reasoning's basics, 46–58
  fallacies to avoid, 66–72
  moral and nonmoral statements and, 58–66
  moral theories and, 79
morality, 13, 162
  religion and, 21–25
moral theories, 78–91
  evaluating of, 84–89
  major theories, 81–84
moral theory, constructing of, 165–78
  considered moral judgments and, 166–67, 174–75
  prima facie principles and, 167–74
  self-evident moral beliefs and, 174–75
moral virtues, 156

N

natural law theory, 83–84, 132–40, 141
  basics and applications of, 132–37
  evaluation of, 137–39
negative rights, 171
neutral standard, critical reasoning and, 23
noncognitivism, 40
nonconsequentialist (deontological) moral theories, 81, 82–84, 120, 155
nonmoral beliefs, 35–36
nonmoral statements, in moral arguments, 59–61, 65–66
nonmoral values, 18
no-rest problem, in utilitarianism, 114–15

normative ethics, 17
norms, dominance of moral norms, 21

O

objectivism, 29
obligations, 18, 79

P

perfect duties, 122, 126–27
Pojman, Louis, 158
positive rights, 171
premises
  in critical reasoning, 19, 48–53
  implicit, 56–58, 61
  in moral arguments, 59–66
prima facie principles, moral theory and, 167–74
problem solving. *See* usefulness, in moral problem solving (Criterion 3)
psychological egoism, 96–99

R

Rawls, John, 145
reason
  natural law theory and, 133–34, 138
  preeminence of, 19
  see also critical reasoning
redistributive justice, 171–72
reflective equilibrium, 81
relativism
  cultural, 30, 32–40
  subjective, 15, 30, 31–32
religion, ethics and morality and, 21–25
rescue, duty of, 173
respect, as prima facie principle, 170–71
rights, positive and negative, 171
Ross, W. D., 169, 171
rule-egoism, 93, 95
rule-utilitarianism, 82, 108, 110, 116–17, 125

S

Sartre, Jean Paul, 24
self-evident statements, 174–75
slippery slope fallacy, 68–69
social contract theory, 141–47

.tes, 24
.nd argument, 53, 62
.ice, Walter T., 33–34
.catements, critical reasoning and, 47–48
straw man fallacy, 71
strong argument, 52–53, 70
subjective relativism, 15, 30, 31–32
subjectivism, 15–16, 79
supererogatory actions, 115, 173

T
Taylor, Paul, 15
teleology. *See* consequentialist moral
    theories
Thompson, Judith Jarvis, 112
tolerance, cultural relativism and,
    36–38

U
universality, categorical imperative
    and, 83, 122–23, 125–28, 129
universalizability, principle of, 19–20
usefulness, in moral problem solving
    (Criterion 3), 88–89

categorical imperative and, 126,
    127–28
ethical egoism and, 100–101
natural law theory and, 135–36, 138
social contract theory and, 144
virtue ethics and, 159
utilitarianism, 79–82, 89, 103–19, 141,
    172
basics and applications of, 103–10
evaluation of, 110–17
utility, principle of, 105, 111

V
valid argument, 51–56, 62
value, theories of, 79
values
    distinguished from obligations, 18
    moral and nonmoral, 14, 18
virtue ethics, 155–64
    basics and applications of, 155–58
    evaluation of, 158–61

W
weak arguments, 52